D1480503

Fighting For Delphine
A Soldier's True Story of Triumph and Tears

LEE BURTMAN

based on the memories of
KEN KRUEGER

Scripture taken from the HOLY BIBLE, NEW INTERNATIONAL VERSION®. Copyright © 1973, 1978, 1984 by International Bible Society. Used by permission of Zondervan Publishing House. All rights reserved.
The "NIV" and "New International Version" trademarks are registered in the United States Patent and Trademark Office by International Bible Society. Use of either trademark requires the permission of International Bible Society.

Image Credits:
Back Cover Photo - Ken Krueger in Paris 1944
Images on pages 8, 11, 68-71, 85, 112, 143, 148, 150, 151 courtesy Ken Krueger
Image on page 77 courtesy Jan Lester
Image on page 295 courtesy Sonia Kuhn
Images marked * are screen captures from the documentary *As Promised*
All other images by Lee Burtman, Greg Burtman

First Printing 2008
Second Edition Printing 2015
ISBN 978-0-692-32000-6

Book Design by KnockOut, LLC   www.knockoutpub.com

Printed in the United States of America

Dedication—

To my dear friend, Ken, who adds to his faith in the Lord the virtues of goodness, knowledge, self-control, perseverance, godliness, brotherly kindness and love (based on 2 Peter 1:5-7). He inspires me and all who are blessed to know him, to do likewise.

$\mathcal{A}$ cknowledgments—

Special thanks to my World War II history consultants, Rick Thompson, Jason Huebscher, and Kyle McMullan who provided their considerable knowledge. Thanks as well to my husband, Greg; my daughters, Bethany and Shana; my mom, Virginia; and dear friends, Jodie Bunish, Anne Johnson, Susan McMullan, Lisa Zimmerlin, and Sam Crabtree, who all took precious time to read, edit, and offer thoughtful comments on the book. They are all special blessings in my life and have played an invaluable role in helping me share Ken's compelling story in the pages of *Fighting for Delphine*.

Preface

On Veteran's Day, Memorial Day, and
Independence Day, the church I attended honored
the brave men and women who served our country
and sacrificed for its people. The veterans were asked to
stand to be recognized with words of thanks, praise, and
heartfelt applause. Each year, as I would gaze around
the room and see the proud yet humble heroes in our
midst, one senior veteran caught my attention. With his
head and shoulders bowed and trembling and with his
hands gripping the chair in front of him, one wondered
what thoughts or memories evoked audible groans and
the plaintive tears surging down his face. Clearly, the
events of more than sixty years ago were still capable of
drawing out deep emotion in this kind and gentle soul.

After one such service acknowledging our
veterans, I approached that gentleman, then eighty-one-
year-old Ken Krueger, and asked him to tell me about
his military service. He gladly did so and each Sunday—

for several months—I enjoyed hearing about his experiences serving in the Army while traveling across Europe during World War II. He also tenderly recalled falling in love for the very first time while stationed in a small town in France. Struck by the detail and drama in his stories, I began to realize that his poignant recollections would make a wonderful book. One day, I felt compelled to ask Ken whether he had ever thought of documenting his stories and if perhaps he would allow me, a novice writer, to do so. Ken responded that he had been praying for many years for someone to help him put his vivid memories into print, primarily to share with family and friends, and that my offer was actually an answer to that prayer!

Over the last ten years, I have had the decided privilege of getting to know Ken and of developing a cherished friendship with him. In reading ninety pages of his honest, touching, often humorous, sometimes gritty, handwritten notes and spending many hours listening to and praying with Ken, I have learned just what those tears he shed during the church tributes represent. It is my honor to share with you Ken's journey of loss and love, of fear and faith, of horror and hope, of triumph and tears, and most of all, of God's grace.

For His glory,
Lee Burtman

Chapter One

*D*elphine. I can't think of a prettier name or one so fitting. I guess it comes from the delphinium flower that grew tall here and there around the weathered house. Her eyes were lavender-blue, just like those delphinium blossoms, but all shiny and clear like the June sky. Her soft, brown hair fell past narrow shoulders and her slim, tanned arms were dark against her yellow dress.

She sure looked pretty standing in the glow of the late afternoon sun. She'd paused a moment to stand and stretch after having gathered basket after basket of deep-purple cabbages from the massive garden. She was *ma petite choute.* How I loved slipping my arms around that tiny waist and holding her close, breathing in her fragrance—such a comfort for a lonesome soldier far from home. How did this nineteen-year-old boy from Minnesota find himself falling in love with a beautiful French girl from Fénétrange, and fighting for her country and his during the second World War?

My story begins and ends humbly enough. I was born in Minneapolis, Minnesota on October 13, 1924, and named Kenneth Alden Krueger. Yes, that would be Friday the 13th. After I was delivered, the doctor came to the waiting room holding a bundle of blue and proudly handed it over to my dad. You can imagine the look on his face when Dad pulled back the blanket and stared into the beautiful face of...a black baby! I guess it's nice to have a doc with a good sense of humor. Thankfully, my dad had one too, so they shared a hardy laugh before I made my true appearance as a bouncing, blue-eyed blonde!

My dad, Charles, had been born in Germany but emigrated to the United States at the age of six. Having been raised on a dairy farm, he was great with horses and had jobs as a logger and as a horse-team driver for the Anheuser-Busch family. Later, he worked at the Mars Candy Company where he met my mom, Florence, who was a candy dipper. Mom had lost her husband, Ole, several years earlier and worked hard to provide for their two daughters. She and my dad married and soon the tiny house they rented for seven dollars a month nearly burst at the seams with my half-sisters, Thurley and Priscilla, yours truly, and my brothers, Russ and Gordy. Though there were few jobs during the Depression, my dad was a hard worker and did whatever he could to take care of us. Dad earned a decent salary working odd jobs, but he drank most of it away, so we had to rent that place—with a garbage dump behind.

Despite frequent attempted visits by residents of the dump (roaches and rats), Mom kept the house immaculate. The soothing smell of fresh bread filled our home twice a week as Mom baked, not just for us, but also for the many tired, hungry wanderers who hitch-hiked to town on the freight trains. They desperately sought work and a place to eat and rest. A sign in the dusty field near us, posted by fellow vagabonds, signaled new visitors where to jump off the train and find a generous family willing to feed them.

Though we had little, Mom always invited them in and shared that wonderful bread, plus butter and homemade jam. My brothers and I never minded walking several miles to downtown Minneapolis to load up our old toy wagon with government surplus commodities, such as flour, sugar and butter. The reward of Mom's special coffee cakes and hot cocoa she'd fix for Saturday nights and Sunday mornings motivated us to make the monthly trek with no complaint.

Having a child's blissful ignorance of the many hardships of those times, my brothers and I lost ourselves in sports, such as ice skating, broom hockey, baseball, track and football. I was quite an athlete but, sad to say, I knocked out my front teeth with that last sport. With neither medical insurance (which cost a whole dollar back then) nor money for repairs, I marched hopefully to a nearby dentist. I stood at his door with bloody nerves and shards of tooth hanging from my mouth, silently praying for help. The dentist took pity on me, yanked out the dangling nerves and told me to go home and let it all heal. I explained that I had no money to offer for his care, but he said that was okay. People then just knew how to help each other.

After several months of covering my ragged grin with my hand when speaking with folks, especially the girls, the dentist could finally finish the repair. He began by drilling holes deep into what was left of my badly-chipped teeth. Believe me, he hadn't pulled out *all* the nerves months before. Next, he hammered gold pegs into the holes and attached pieces of porcelain to the pegs to fill in the gaps, kind of like a jigsaw puzzle. Those teeth were really sturdy; I used them until I was fifty-seven years old! Striving to be fair and honest in all things, I took a job at a local grocery to begin paying back the nice dentist. Later, I completely paid off the eighty dollar fee with my meager military salary of thirty dollars a month.

Even more important to me than sports was my faith. I remember my mom, a devoted Christian, teaching me the Bible; as a young child I accepted Jesus as my Savior. But it wasn't until the age of sixteen, after I'd attended a revival meeting at First Baptist Church of Minneapolis in 1940, that I dedicated my life to following and serving God. The outspoken evangelist, Mordecai Ham, had come to the Twin Cities after having held soul-winning crusades, mainly in southern states, for many years.

Thousands upon thousands heard the Gospel and became believers through Ham's ministry. Perhaps the most well-known evangelist of modern time, Billy Graham, was saved at one of Ham's rallies in Charlotte, North Carolina in November of 1934, at the age of sixteen. Both men have been an example to me since then, along with that other great evangelist, the Apostle Paul, who declared, "I am not ashamed of the gospel, because it is the *power* of God for the salvation of everyone who believes" (Romans 1:16, emphasis added). I praise God for that gospel power in my life—it would be called upon and trusted in so many times in the days and years to come.

On December 7th, 1941, my dad came home from Gil's Bar, his usual watering hole, and announced that the Japanese had just bombed Pearl Harbor. He looked at me with tears in his eyes and in his voice and said, "Ken, they're going to take you." He meant, of course, "Uncle Sam." I'm not sure what shocked me more: news of the attack or my dad's emotional statement. You see, I never felt he cared that much about me. For years, up until we could defend ourselves, my dad would beat me and my brothers nearly every day. He'd come home drunk and angry and beat my mom awhile, then get us boys. I got the brunt of it, being the oldest and biggest kid. So it was kind of a nice surprise to see those tears and know that he really did love me.

A few months later, a bunch of guys from our neighborhood suggested we all join the military, even though none of us had quite finished high school. We went down to the local draft board to sign up, requesting that we be assigned to the same branch of service. The recruiters assured us that we'd be kept together; the truth is, I never saw any of those guys again until after the war—the ones who made it home, anyway.

We soon received a letter telling us to report to the Minneapolis Armory. Hundreds of men were there when we arrived, being sworn in, and then taken to Fort Snelling, where over 300,000 people would begin their military service. The production line was next—the process where we were stripped not only of our clothes but of our families, our freedom, our very selves.

We removed our civilian clothes then walked down the hall, in all our glory, to another room where we were given identical uniforms and haircuts. We were then instructed to lift two heavy pails of sand and stand on a measuring device to determine the length and width of our feet. The now-bulging feet would be close to the size they'd be later on when we'd be loaded down with gear as soldiers. Footwear came only in sizes nine and eleven. Heaven help those with anything different! Later, I heard that some men in other regiments didn't even receive combat boots, as I had, until near the end of the war. Those soldiers often suffered from something much like frostbite, called "Trench Foot." The plain shoes they'd been issued at induction didn't protect them from the cold, wet conditions found in the trenches and muddy fields of Europe. Their feet would turn ghostly white and numb, with some men losing toes to gangrene. A dead soldier's boots became a great treasure for a GI who had none. Warm, dry combat boots were finally issued in the last months of the war, but only to men in the rear echelon—the Army must have figured that those fighting in the front lines wouldn't need fancy boots for long.

Shuffling along to the next station, we were given a series of painful shots and vaccinations in each arm. A few guys passed out at the very sight of the shiny needles. I wondered how long they'd last on the battlefield. We were all herded into a large room, still clothes-less and clue-less. You should have seen that motley group: every size, shape, color, height, and weight you could imagine. God certainly must have a great sense of humor!

After having been given physical and psychiatric tests, we were fingerprinted, issued an eight-digit serial number, allowed to dress and required to sign induction papers. I was suddenly and finally in the military! A buddy and I were hoping to get into the Navy or Marines or maybe even the Paratroopers; but once the officials saw that my friend had a bad case of blemishes, he was turned down. The Army was the only branch that would take him. I had passed scrutiny with flying colors (fortunate to have a good complexion!) and could have joined any outfit. However, I chose to enter the Army with my pal—only to be quickly separated for the duration of our military careers. After learning I had been to mechanics school and had raised homing pigeons, the Army ordered me to be trained at Signal Corps Camp.

The new inductees were housed for a week in the barracks at Fort Snelling. Before being sent to training, we received passes to visit our families for a single day. We joined a huge throng of fellow soldiers heading home, some for the last time ever. Hundreds of GIs shoved their way into the street cars, nearly crushing each other. The men were jammed together so tightly that, while entering the car, I lifted my legs off the ground and the press of the mob carried me several feet!

I recall walking up the crumbling sidewalk of our old house, so proud and eager to show my family my uniform—now slightly rumpled but still crisp from being new. After hugs, kisses, and not a few tears from my mom and sisters, it was time to head back to the barracks. I never saw my dad during the brief visit— guess he was still at Gil's Bar.

The streets were nearly deserted and dark, except for the yellow glow of the arc lights overhead. They shed just enough light to help you find your way. Walking slowly along, I thought back to the time I was sixteen years old and had dedicated myself to following God. If I was to be faithful to that promise, I would need to learn to rely on His light to lead me through the dark days ahead.

*"Your word is a lamp to my feet
and a light to my path"*
(Psalm 119:105).

Chapter Two

M*isery***.** I'll bet you've heard people say
Missouri that way. Well, we soldiers at Camp
Crowder like to think we invented that pronunciation.
Misery sure tells you how we felt about that state *and*
basic training camp.

The first thing I learned there was what the term
"GI" meant: <u>G</u>overnment <u>I</u>ssue. In other words, the
Army owned you. *All* of you. Our initiation to military
life began with an invasion—by the dentist. I'm not sure
what they were looking for, but they poked, prodded,
scraped and scrubbed every square inch of every tooth
for two solid days! Then we suffered another sort of
invasion.

Late one night, while each Company barracks
was buzzing with fifty snoring men, the lights suddenly
snapped on. We were ordered, in no uncertain terms,
to get up immediately, take off our shorts and dress
in nothing but a raincoat and a pair of boots. We were

forbidden to use the bathroom and told to line up and leave the building. We all sprang up and followed those orders, wondering what was up but not daring to ask. The whole Company marched to the recreation room in one very long line, joining hundreds of equally-stunned soldiers.

Our eyes, stinging from the glaring light, took in a familiar form: the Company doctor, sitting on a low stool. Each guy, most just young like me, had to step forward, open his coat for the doctor, and (I'll try to be delicate here) present his "family jewels" in such a way that the doc could see any sign of venereal disease. Most of us were still "clean" at this point—but that would change with time and circumstance. The unfortunate few who failed were yanked out of line and quickly shipped to the hospital, where they stayed until cured.

VD was a serious, relentless problem for the military, even though they tried hard to fight it. In Louisiana, I saw the tall, wire fences of the "chicken farms" where hundreds of civilian women ("chicks") were quarantined and treated for their venereal diseases. In Europe, the medics even ran brothels for the soldiers to ensure that the girls were healthy and the guys were happy. At camp we were shown gross films of actual men who suffered from syphilis and gonorrhea. I hate to say it, but trying to scare the pants *on* us didn't work too well; there were just too many dames here and across Europe more than willing to comfort a scared, lonesome soldier who had a few bucks and a pass in his pocket. Anyway, that night I felt bad for my new buddies. They looked sort of dazed and too tired to be indignant, while stumbling back in the dark to their cots for a couple more winks. I can't imagine the whole thing was much fun for that doctor, either. As I said: misery.

At Camp Crowder, one lesson we had to learn, without fail, was how to be neat and orderly. Man, I

thought my mom ran a tight ship. She was no match, though, for the sergeants who trained and inspected us. We were taught how to make a bed so tight that the mattress bowed up at the edges. You were required to be able to literally bounce a coin off it! The Sarge would even scrutinize the bottom of the mattress—just one tiny wrinkle in the sheet and he would make you rip it all off and start over until it was perfect, no matter how many tries it took.

Everything inside your foot locker, such as socks and underwear, had to be rolled and placed in a certain order. Clothes had to be crisply pressed, every button buttoned, every zipper zipped, and every garment hung in a certain sequence. You were issued two pairs of shoes, which had to be buffed until you could almost see your face in the leather, and then placed under a certain corner of the bed. We were warned to alternate wearing each set of shoes so both pairs would be good and broken-in. Some poor saps ignored the rule so they could keep one pair looking spiffy. If they got caught, though, they were made to wear the newer shoes while on a long hike. Walking around later with no skin left on your heels would serve as a painful lesson in obedience.

Morning would arrive early at boot camp, even before the sun did. We'd be startled awake by a bugle blaring "Reveille." We had our own words to that familiar tune: "I hate to get up, I hate to get up, I hate to get up in the moooor-ning!" We'd dash to the bathroom to shave, shower, then get dressed and make that bed—perfectly. The next bugle tune, the assembly call, told us we had to fall out in our platoons and stand at attention for roll call. The corporal would bark out each soldier's name and, when everyone had been accounted for, we'd march to the mess hall for breakfast while the mess call sounded. The words we made up to that tune were:

"Soupy, soupy, soupy, without a single bean.
Coffee, coffee, coffee, tastin' mighty green.
Porky, porky, porky, without a strip of lean!"

As the men dutifully filed in, they'd sit in the same order in which they'd been marching and quickly, efficiently fill each bench. Usually a quick study, I learned to worm my way to the end of the line and sit at the last table, often holding fewer men and more food and milk!

You quickly learned to use those manners your mom tried so hard to teach you—if you wanted anything to eat. "Please" and "thank you" were necessary to get a dish passed to you. If someone dared to "short-stop" the dish, that is, grab something off it as it was passed, the person asking for the dish had permission to give the food to the "grabber": right in his face! I hated to do that, though (what a waste of those warm, gloppy potatoes). The guys also avoided being the last one to polish off the food in a bowl. That chump had to quit filling his face for a moment and take the bowl over to the cooks for a refill. Most guys were way too hungry and lazy to want to do that.

After chow, it was time to practice marching as a platoon. I felt like a dummy since it took me awhile to figure out the commands like, "Get to the rear march." The sergeant, having observed this, singled me out and drilled me separately until I got it. I finally became so good at marching that sometimes the Sarge even made me our platoon leader, and I was the one giving the orders! Then it was on to the rifle range. I'd never even held a gun, let alone shot one, but quickly learned after target shooting day after day. I was pretty good at that, too, and made the rank of "marksman." Feeling rather smug about my new-found talents, I approached machine gun training with little fear. I was soon humbled, though, by the zing of real machine gun bullets zipping by mere inches over my head, as I crawled through a deep, muddy trench. The barrage continued as I scrambled across a smoke-filled field with dynamite blasting all around and dirt and soot choking me and burning my eyes. Then I had to flip over onto my back and continue scooting under barbed wire, which scraped and snagged my uniform. Later, some men realized that the barbs had also torn jagged channels down their foreheads, which had quickly filled with scarlet blood. Of course, you didn't dare stand up until you were well beyond the long row of machine gun stands spitting ammo at you. We couldn't believe one guy who jumped up too early on the training course and was accidentally shot, then whisked to the hospital— guess he ran into a snake as he was crawling on his belly in the trench!

Another thing I'd never held was a steering wheel. Here I was a trainee in mechanics school, learning to tear apart and rebuild vehicles, yet I couldn't drive one! Dad had never kept enough money to own a car. So when I found myself sitting in the driver's seat of a one-and-a-half-ton truck and being ordered by a lieutenant to "double-clutch" it, I panicked and failed the test miserably.

Amazingly, just a few months later, I'd find myself as a motor messenger in Europe. I'll never forget how my sweaty hands felt, desperately gripping the wheel of that jeep (slang for "general purpose" vehicle), while driving down foreign roads in utter darkness and dodging German Stukas. Those dive bombers would literally scream around you as they dropped their lethal five-hundred-pound bombs. I'd race blindly in the night, fiercely determined to deliver the critical messages entrusted to me while being equally terrified of German snipers, whose well-aimed bullets pierced the blackness. God protected me from harm in a miraculous way, but more about that later.

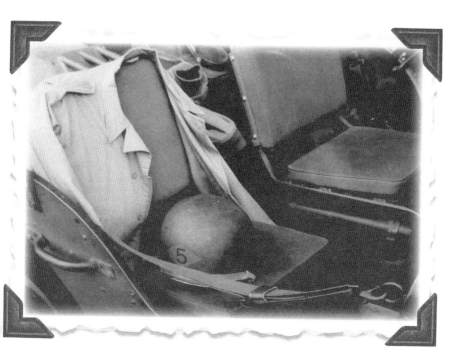

Despite the new buddies I'd made at camp and all the excitement of training, I felt painfully lonely and sad. I had never been away from home before, let alone for three months. One time, I walked alone in the cool night air to the top of a hill that overlooked the city of Neosho. Its sparkling lights scattered across the dark horizon reminded me of home in Minneapolis. I stood there a long time and just cried.

Chapter Three

L ousy. That would describe the next three months. One morning we were ordered to get up even earlier than usual, pack up all our belongings and head toward the train station. With boot camp behind us, we were all being sent to different outfits for more specialized training. If we thought Missouri lived up to its nickname, we hadn't yet spent time in "Lousy-ana!"

We stood around the station waiting for hours (one of the many times we had to "hurry up and wait") in hundred degree temperatures and a hot drizzle of rain, until the officer-in-charge took pity on us and bought tickets for a movie show. Just as we were enjoying the relative cool of the dark theater, our coach arrived, plunging us once again into the blazing heat and humidity. We struggled to pry open the rusted windows of the old car, only to let in a steamy blast laced with engine smoke—but it felt better anyhow. As I glanced out the misty window, I saw a man who looked to be walking in slow motion. It seemed to take minutes before one foot hit the pavement and the other was lifted up: it was so dang hot, no wonder he walked so slowly.

The train took its sweat-drenched cargo to Leesville, Louisiana where Army trucks delivered us to the 92nd Signal Battalion, next to Camp Polk. I was placed in the HQ & HQ Company and assigned to an eight-man-squad tent with a wooden floor and mosquito netting protecting each cot. Now I was used to the voracious mosquitoes we grew in Minnesota, but I was really thankful for that netting, because those suckers down south were about the size of dragonflies! The cots were adequate enough but the thin blanket you were issued sure wasn't. You'd nearly boil during the day but need your heavy overcoat thrown on top of you to survive the damp, chilly nights.

Even taking into account the hellish weather, the day after arriving I started feeling as if I were burning up. My head began throbbing deeply and then my body chimed in with aches and shivers. I tried to shrug it off, but keeping up with calisthenics and running track in that condition was impossible. I had been on the track team at Boys Vocational High School back in Minneapolis and could usually run for hours without tiring. Now I could barely keep up with the last guy on the field and had to quit.

After checking myself into sick bay, a medic took my temperature and then sent me back to my tent to lie down. When he re-checked me later, he immediately called the doctor, who took me by ambulance to the hospital. I lay there in nothing but shorts in a large ward with a dozen beds that were covered in cool, white sheets. Ice packs lay heavily on my head and were stuffed under my arm pits. A nurse continually swabbed my body in an effort to cool me down—the smell of rubbing alcohol stung my nose.

While in a feverish stupor one night, I hazily recall a lot of commotion near the bathroom. Some guy in my ward had tried to hang himself from the stall doorframe. You could see his feet dangling and tapping the floor like a marionette, with pale arms limp at his sides. I later heard that the hospital staff had revived him: he'd been going for a "Section-8." He was hoping, short of dying, to be declared nuts enough to be discharged from the Army. Guess he'd had enough already.

I remained in the hospital for more than two weeks, recovering from some ailment never revealed to me. All I knew was that I nearly went to Glory, but God had other plans for me. Although I started feeling better, the nurse kept insisting on my drinking this nasty-tasting medicine. When she wasn't looking, I'd pour the vile stuff into a flower vase! I managed to improve without it and was finally returned to my battalion.

Having been placed in the motor pool doing maintenance, such as greasing vehicles and changing oil, I was able to practice my driving, which was sorely needed. The other guys working with me were nice enough, although I was troubled by their constant swearing, talking dirty about women, gambling away their pay and bragging about getting drunk. I suppose those things were considered to be an accepted part of Army life, but the Bible taught me in Ephesians four and five not to let any unwholesome talk come out of my mouth. Listening to those foul mouths all day was demoralizing, so I asked the captain of the motor pool if I could be transferred. Since I had finally passed my driver's test and was now skilled at handling anything from a jeep to a ten-ton truck, I was eligible to be a motor messenger and was chosen to do so. This would be great experience for the service I'd perform in the near future—delivering mail and messages across Europe. Such correspondence was often crucial to the execution of the war.

My jeep training began after sunset as I learned to drive with no lights, up and down steep hills, through smelly swamps, over sandy plains, and across bridges made of just two railroad ties and a few wood planks. At times, the only way to stay on the road was to look up toward the deep navy sky and use the gap between the tree tops as my visual guide. It was quite a feat not to hit a pig or a cow along the way. The animals had open range and were often found dotting the roads, bloody and stiff, in the daylight.

One time, near twilight, the carnage was human. While practicing my driving, a police car zipped by me. A few miles later, I came upon the reason for his haste: a car carrying soldiers had run into a semi-trailer gas truck. Earlier, a delivery truck had gone off the road to avoid one of those wandering cows and had tipped over in a ditch. The semi driver had stopped to help and had left his vehicle at an angle in the road. The car, full of drunk GIs, came along and rammed the gas truck, seriously injuring them all. I stopped to help pick up one boy who was not much older than me. His body was so limp that it took four of us to set him in the ambulance. I paused briefly to pray for him, but it was too late: he'd gone on to meet the Lord. I just hoped he knew Him as his Savior. I'll never forget the feeling of that young man's still-warm body in my arms. It was the first time I'd seen a man die—wish it were the last.

My one and only furlough was granted after I'd been in the Army for six months. It took two days to get home by train, but I didn't mind too much as there was a pretty girl on board. We never spoke but flirted a bit with glances, winks and smiles until her stop in Missouri. I wanted to say something but there seemed no point as I was soon heading back to camp. The time at home rushed by so fast that the next thing I knew, I was back on the train, clutching a bag of ham sandwiches from Mom. Boy, were they good to this homesick soldier, but not as good as seeing the faces of my mom and sisters again.

Soon after returning to Camp Polk, the 92nd Battalion was ordered to move to Paris: Paris, Texas, that is! I felt honored to be chosen to drive the 1st Lieutenant there and to remain his personal driver, as well as the driver for the entire HQ & HQ Company while at Camp Maxey. I was allowed to bunk in the enlisted men's barracks and, since the jeep and I had to always be available to my superiors, I avoided the drudgery of drills, marches and the dreaded KP duty. Peeling, cutting, boiling, and mashing potatoes for over two hundred men, then scrubbing the kitchen until it gleamed, was not my idea of fun!

I did have to take my turn at guard duty, though, using the 45 Thompson machine gun ("Tommy gun") I'd been issued. It was mine to keep track of throughout the war and learn to assemble, take apart and keep immaculate. We'd practice shooting our guns, containing real ammo, into the buildings of a "town" set-up, or at plywood enemy soldiers that would jump out at us from deep in the woods. I became a really good shot and made "expert" with the machine gun. These practices (and a few later in Normandy, France) were the only times I'd ever fire my gun throughout the entire war.

As a guard you had to learn ten commands and be ready and able to recite them perfectly at any moment. While on duty you were not to obey anyone but the Corporal of the Guard, the Sergeant of the Guard, or the Officer of the Day. You had to remain at your post, no matter what, until relieved by another guard or be subject to a court-martial. In war you could be shot for abandoning your post.

Each person approaching you had to stop immediately upon hearing your command to halt, and then identify themselves— or face the consequences. I heard about the night a captain was coming toward the guard of the motor pool and was ordered to halt. The captain just kept walking so the guard hollered "halt" a second time. He continued forward despite a third order to halt and marched up to the guard, who swung his rifle butt up and hit the captain right in the chin, knocking him out cold and parting him from a few of his teeth. The captain could have been shot for his refusal to stop, but no bullets were allowed in our rifles, except during training. While the captain recovered in the hospital, the guard was sent to a different outfit so the captain could not retaliate against him later.

The order came: Companies A, B, C, and HQ & HQ were to be shipped overseas. We celebrated with a special party, boarded the troop trains, and headed for New York, spending three days traveling. We were housed at Camp Shanks for a few days and then transported again by train to a big rail yard. There we were loaded down with a large barracks bag labeled with our name and serial number, and with our heavy overcoat, helmet and weapons. We had to carry all this gear over railroad tracks for several blocks to reach our ship, the USS *Anne Arundel*. We were thankful for the women of the Red Cross who greeted us at the gang plank with hot coffee, doughnuts and good wishes.

Once on the ship, we found our hanging canvas bunks, stacked four high with mine being second to the top. It took all day to load the 92nd Battalion, but at 5:00 p.m. we were finally towed away from the dock. Two hours later we heard her engines rumbling awake. You could feel the huge ship trembling as she slowly traversed the harbor, headed for where God only knew. An icy wind blew across the deck, chilling our bodies but not our spirits. It was December 18, 1943.

Chapter Four

*O*ver *There.*
Over there, over there
    Send the word, send the word
    Over there,
    That the Yanks are coming
    The Yanks are coming
    The drums rum-tumming everywhere.
    So prepare, say a prayer
    Send the word, send the word
    To beware.
    We'll be over, we're coming over
    And we won't be back till it's over
    Over there!

That old George M. Cohan song, written during
the First World War, ran through my mind as we set sail.
Yes, the Yanks were coming, but it sure seemed to take
forever to get *over there*. Three weeks of swaying and
bouncing across the Atlantic would feel like three years

to our stomachs! It took twelve days alone to reach our rendezvous point about fifty miles east of Boston.

We joined a convoy of nearly three dozen ships: a battleship, aircraft carriers, destroyers, tankers, and troopships. Our first challenge: to safely cross "Torpedo Alley." This area of the Atlantic stretched from near Newfoundland in the north, to the Outer Banks of North Carolina in the south. "Wolf Packs," death squads of fifteen to twenty German submarines, prowled those waters. Their objective was to take down merchant ships loaded with supplies, food, oil, and sadly, civilians. And they were very good at it. From January until July of 1942 alone, German U-boats sank 397 ships, killing over 5,000 people. They proudly called it "Happy Time" or the "Great American Turkey Shoot." Of course, destroying troopships was an even greater prize to the enemy. We heard of ships carrying soldiers which had been sunk in "Torpedo Alley" before our convoy passed through and wondered quietly to ourselves whether we would be the next "turkeys."

During the voyage, I was very glad that I volunteered for gun duty. A 37mm anti-aircraft gun platform sat five floors up from the boiler room at the top of a heat shaft. I worked and slept on the metal grate of the platform which, though not exactly comfortable, was a warm respite from the cold and stench of the barracks below. Down in the "hole," as we called it, the smell of vomit mingled with the Pine-Sol used to clean up after seasick soldiers. (To this day, some sixty years later, even the thought of that cleaner makes me ill!)

While performing midnight watch on the gun platform, I always accepted offers of hot coffee or soup and crackers, despite feeling a bit sick myself. I never missed a meal in the mess hall, either. Eating there was quite an experience! With no chairs to be had, we'd grab food off large platters and eat as we walked single-file the length of chest-high tables. Here and there someone would lose their lunch, so to speak, across the table, but we just kept moving and eating like nothing had happened. The "head" or toilet room at the front of the ship was a popular place for the sick men. There were two long pipes on either side of the room with a dozen stools spaced every three feet on each pipe. Iron rails let you hang on for dear life as you took care of business, often at both ends.

Gusty winds and rough waves, which often washed right over the ship's bow, were the reason for all this discomfort. Those waves got so high at times that when the ship would go down in a swell, you could see nothing but a wall of blue-green water surrounding you. Next, the ship would rise on top of the wave, and you could see down to all kinds of vessels below. One time at the top of a swell, I was glad to see the USS *Texas* near us. A heavily armored and armed battleship, she protected us and the smaller destroyers in our convoy. The destroyers, or "tin cans," didn't need a whole lot of help, though. They were so fast they could ditch enemy subs as well as deliver depth charges to wipe them out.

When the seas were especially dangerous, we rarely went on deck. If ordered to go atop, we'd grasp onto special ropes and twist on the red flashlight attached to our life jackets. If you were unfortunate enough to fall overboard, the ship would not stop. If you were fortunate enough to remain afloat, an alert was relayed to a destroyer whose crew would look for your little red light, find you bobbing in the water, and then pluck you from the icy sea.

After awhile, the men got used to the heaving waves and stopped heaving so much themselves. Instead of stark white faces and black whiskers, they looked at each other with colorful, sun-burned cheeks and clean-shaven faces. The guys passed the time playing cards, gambling, and watching the antics of the dolphins that swam and played alongside the ship as she sliced through the water. The soldiers also enjoyed smoking, but had to be extra careful not to light up on deck after dark and risk alerting the enemy about our position. They told us you could see the glow of a cigarette from miles away. Every evening we'd hear the boatman's whistle piercing the air to signal the "no smoking" time—in a collective groan, the men would take a deep, final drag and reluctantly mash their precious smokes onto the ship's deck.

I liked looking out across the ocean on a calm night with a full moon glistening across serene water. If you scanned all around you, it seemed that the ship was in the middle of a great circle and the ocean just curved away, like being on the top of a big ball. We were an easy target for the German subs on those nights, but God, in His sovereign plan, continued to protect us as we drew closer to our destination and our destiny.

Chapter Five

 ritish Isles. On January 7, 1944 we
saw the southern coast of Ireland, but we kept
going through the Irish Sea to stop briefly in Liverpool,
England and drop off some of the troops and supplies.
We set sail again and headed for Belfast. Northern
Ireland played a vital role in assisting the allied forces.
Londonderry, northwest of Belfast, was a base for the
Battle of the Atlantic. The Royal British Navy, U.S.
Navy, and Royal Canadian Navy warships operated from
there.

We unloaded the ship and then boarded trains
for the trip to Lurgan, Ireland, a small town forty miles
southwest of Belfast. Lurgan was considered a "white"
town. In those days, whites and blacks were segregated
in the Army. Whites were placed in fighting units, and
blacks were assigned to truck-driving outfits. This had
to do with unfounded rumors during WWI that blacks
tended to run away from combat. The truth is that in
both World Wars, African-Americans demonstrated

bravery, loyalty and ability in combat, often without proper training or adequate equipment. And the "combat failure" (desertion) rate was similar to that of white soldiers. Blacks did distinguish themselves, too, as the truck drivers and front-line support they were considered. The famed "Red Ball Express," a massive supply effort that was crucial to the defeat of Nazi Germany, was made up of nearly all African-American drivers. Over six thousand trucks and trailers transported more than four hundred thousand tons of essential matériel to American troops, as they advanced across France from Normandy to the German border between August and November of 1944.

We were housed in seventy-five Quonset huts at the edge of town, each holding twelve to fifteen men. Our beds were made of two short saw horses with boards over them. A burlap bag filled with straw was our mattress. Such luxury was supplied by the British government—for a fee. I learned the hard way not to punch up your bed for the night. The next morning I woke up with itchy, red bites all over my body: fleas. We called them "cooties" and had a song for them:

"C-C-C-Cootie, C-C-C-Cootie,
You're the only bug that I abhor.
When the moon shines, over the bunkhouse,
I'll be scratching until my back is sore!"

They were tough little buggers. Once, I caught one and squeezed it to death, or so I thought. When I opened my hand to examine my prey, it popped right out like a tiny spring and happily sprang away! I got hold of some DDT powder and sprinkled it all over my bed, which, thankfully, took care of the problem.

We marveled at the brilliant green landscape—in January! Cottages with green thatched roofs dotted the lush, emerald countryside, while dry-stone walls crisscrossed the land for miles. Rather than having gates, those walls were made without mortar, so that a farmer could take apart a section of the wall to let his herds pass into another field. The wall was then built back up, stone by stone. Every road, no matter how small or insignificant, was paved with black top. The people drove their sheep and cows right through the towns on those roads. Every hill was terraced and made into a colorful step garden. Tidy rows of cabbage, kale, chard, chicory, leeks and potatoes would feed hungry families through the winter. Peat bogs stretched out as far as the eye could see and narrow rectangles of cut peat or "turf" were set in stacks to dry, then burned as fuel to heat cottages.

In the midst of this beautiful setting were very practical considerations as well: outhouses. A big bucket sat under each wooden seat of our camp latrine to collect the waste. Every so often, a woman driving a big horse-drawn wagon would come by our camp and empty those buckets into a large barrel. Then the horse would trudge back down the road with the woman and her treasure. We called that rig the "honey wagon." Nice job, don't you think? We appreciated her efforts and the collection served as fertilizer in those pretty countryside gardens. One time we stopped at Army headquarters located in a castle. As we were allowed to use the facilities, I was surprised to see lovely paintings—in the toilets! The insides of the bowls were expertly painted with colorful designs—a lot more charming than those Army latrines.

The people of Ireland were charming, also. A sweet lady in the local market sold me some tea and sugar, although they were strictly rationed. Smuggling of restricted goods from the Irish Free State or Éire, in the south, to Northern Ireland, known as Ulster, was not uncommon. In fact, there were stories of slim women taking the train from Belfast heading south to Dublin who returned from there looking very much in a "family way." In reality, they carried tea, sugar and bacon in their fake swollen bellies. Other females left Ulster looking as though they were expecting and returned to the North carrying their "babies" of ham or roasted turkey wrapped in shawls! The customs officials began to crack down on these practices, especially after they became suspicious of the many frequent funeral processions that crossed the border from the South to the North. If a march was stopped and the casket examined, the officials would often find cold cuts rather than a cold corpse inside!

I was very glad to meet some fellow Christians in Lurgan as I listened to a group of them preaching about Jesus on a street corner. They were so kind in inviting me to their homes and treating me as a brother in Christ. I'll never forget them or their hospitality. I also won't forget the P38 that buzzed us while at the barracks. The P38 Lightning was our special fighter boasting a dual-fuselage structure and air speeds over four hundred miles per hour. She flew at high altitudes, allowing her to dive down on the German planes flying below and to bomb enemy tanks on the ground. Anyway, it was an awesome sight and sound the first time she thundered overhead, just above the tree tops, then shot up and disappeared into the vast blue sky.

Now it was time to begin what I'd been trained for: delivering messages by vehicle across Europe. There was only one problem; In Ireland, England, Scotland, and Wales, they drive on the other side of the road! Their vehicles are equipped for this with steering wheels on the right. But our American jeeps had their wheels on the left, of course, so it took some getting used to. I was nearly killed one day as a buddy of mine was driving a jeep and tried to pass a large truck in front of us as we drove in the left lane. From my vantage point in the right-side passenger seat, I could see a huge, red double-decker bus barreling toward us in the right lane, but my buddy, steering from the left side of the jeep, couldn't! As he veered into the path of the oncoming bus, my ear-piercing screams told him in no uncertain terms that he'd better pull back immediately into our own lane! That he did and our jeep miraculously missed a head-on collision with just inches to spare.

It was such a close call that the bus driver jerked his vehicle to an abrupt stop at the side of the road and stumbled down the steps, pale as a ghost, to check for any damage. Thanks be to God for His protection.

I remember one of the first times I drove in Ireland. After nearly spinning out on black ice (impossible to see on those pitch-black roads), I had a serious accident. I was heading up a hill and around a curve with another buddy at about fifty miles an hour, when a car appeared in my lane. I hit her hard, shearing the bumper, radiator, wheel, fender and hood right off her car! After the sickening jolt and stunned silence that followed, I realized I couldn't move. My knees had been jammed into the dashboard, and my stomach was nearly impaled by the steering wheel. My buddy, who had flown over the windshield when I'd slammed on the brakes, lay motionless on the pavement. I glanced over to see two Irish women in the other car, covered in broken eggs and blood. I have a vague memory of someone stopping to help and of the jeep being towed away.

Once again, I, and the others, would be protected by God's mighty hand and survive the collision. Later, I had to appear in Irish court to determine who was at fault; the United States chose not to press charges against the woman, who had been driving in the wrong lane, accompanied by her sister and a week's worth of farm-fresh eggs!

Another night, I hit a big dog. The only lights we could use in the dark were "cat eyes": small, white lights on the fender that cast a thin, flat beam. With those as my only guide, I didn't see the poor pup heading toward me. I tried so hard to avoid him once I finally caught sight of him running into my path. I cringed hearing that "thwump" sound as the bumper slammed into his side. At least it was quick. I stroked the silky fur at the scruff of his neck and then gently lifted him and set him on the side of the road. He was a nice, old boy; someone was going to miss him.

At night, the lights had to be out everywhere in Northern Ireland, including the Army base. Walking guard duty was a frightening prospect, as we had to patrol the dark fields in back of the Quonset huts. Most guys on duty just stood around in groups, rather than head out alone on foot patrol. It would have been very easy for the Germans to attack us at our isolated position on the end of town. However, there was no direct fighting there. The Germans cleverly chose to infiltrate the town during the day. Using perfect Irish accents and disguises, they obtained secret information and passwords, and then relayed that intelligence to their buddies. Since it was known there were so many Nazi spies in Ireland, it was also rumored that we were going to invade the Irish Free State to stop the espionage. The rumors were unfounded, but the American guards on base were actually issued bullets, just in case. (They usually performed their duty without ammunition!)

The food in Ireland took some getting used to, especially the thick, canned milk I had to use on my cereal. The powdered eggs weren't too bad to me, but some guys hated them. I also didn't mind the creamed chipped-beef on toast, which had a nasty nickname I won't share here. At least the food at the mess hall was better than what we'd have later on the battlefield: "K" rations. The box would contain those powdered eggs, hard biscuits, coffee, and sugar for breakfast and cheese and crackers with Kool-Aid for dinner. If you were lucky, you'd get "C" rations or cans containing beans, vegetable hash or stew, and some crackers. I heard about some units having nothing to eat but Spam for breakfast, lunch and dinner. Then those lucky guys would receive care packages from home filled with, guess what? More Spam! We did receive an occasional chocolate or fruit bar, which sure tasted good to this boy, who sorely missed his mom's good cooking! Sometimes I'd dream about her delicious pork chops or fried chicken and wake up feeling more homesick than ever.

Toilet paper came in the boxes or cans, too. At first it was the usual white stuff, but later in the war the "tp" and the cans it came in were olive drab, so we wouldn't alert the enemy about our positions with our refuse.

In mid-May we were visited by none other than George S. Patton. I remember him smiling and saluting a soldier who had climbed a telephone pole to salute the general upon his arrival in Lurgan. Although Patton did not address the nine hundred troops then (he would do so later in England), he spoke briefly to the Lieutenant Colonel of our battalion, advising him to keep any extra soldiers he might have: they would be needed in France.

We soon knew something was up. Each messenger jeep was assigned an officer possessing sealed envelopes to be delivered to every outfit in Northern Ireland. Those outfits quickly began to move out, as did ours. We were heading to England, while on our way to the beaches of Normandy. On May 23, 1944 we loaded up and convoyed to Belfast, where we'd take the ferry across the Irish Sea to Scotland. After we'd driven our vehicles onto the ferry, we had some time to see the harbor. A British sub was docked there, and we were allowed to explore the cramped rooms on board. It was interesting to see how the sailors lived and worked, but it made me very glad to be in the Army!

After arriving in Stranraer, we unloaded the vehicles and lined up in another huge convoy, with the larger trucks in the front and the jeeps holding up the rear. The Scottish countryside was beautiful, and we enjoyed snaking our way through the valleys, climbing steep hills, and then flying down the other side. Along the way, we stopped at British camps to rest and eat.

Well, I should qualify that. We *tried* to eat. The food was so greasy that most of our soldiers stated that they weren't *that* hungry and simply threw away the musty, old potatoes and slimy gravy. The only edible things were the ham and chocolate bars with nuts. Sure wish I'd tried the classic specialty of the area—fish 'n chips— but never did the entire time I was there! I'm sure the British thought we were terribly wasteful. However, the saddest thing was that, no matter how awful the provision, the American government was charged for every meal, for every bed, for every soldier.

Soon after arriving in Oxford, England we were aware of further sealed orders having been delivered to each division and unit. Although we weren't told the nature of the orders, the next event confirmed our suspicions that it was time. We were ordered to drive to a huge field where thousands upon thousands of men slowly gathered over several hours. Suddenly, General Patton appeared on a large platform to address the troops. I could barely see him over the sea of heads in front of me, but I sure could hear him. His voice boomed loud and clear over the loudspeakers as he told us how to kill the enemy: "Don't just shoot the Germans but cut out their living guts and use them to grease tank treads." (Later in the war, the American GIs would call him "blood and guts"—his guts but *our* blood.) His theory was to always move forward and "go like h***." He was described as tough, arrogant and profane. True to form, about every third word was a curse word. I wondered what the people in the city thought as they heard his nonstop swearing over the speakers.

After his speech, he was driven to each unit, holding onto the windshield with his left hand and saluting the troops with his right. His famous ivory pistols sparkled while dangling at his sides. Soon he disappeared in a cloud of brown dust billowing from the back of his vehicle as it sped away from the city. As we marched back to our jeeps, shoulder-to-shoulder, I wondered how many of these men would survive the invasion of France. Would I?

Before sailing to France, I was able to see many cities in England while delivering messages: London, Birmingham, Stratford-upon-Avon, and Coventry. Although Coventry was considered the most bombed-out city in England, later on I'd hear that its condition was nothing compared to the devastation of some of the German cities that had been leveled by the Allies.

In London I saw the Thames River and Big Ben, as well as the famous London fog, which seemed to swallow me up whole! I was amazed by the citizens on the misty streets there who didn't run or even flinch when the sirens began to wail and an explosion was heard. They were either hardened to the threat or may have simply decided to deny the enemy the pleasure of disrupting the everyday pace and peace of English life.

One of the hardest things for me to see as I traveled was the solemn look on the children's faces. They weren't as stoic as the people in London. One day, after returning from a message run to Wales, my buddy and I pulled over to the side of the road to talk with a group of little kids. When we handed them huge oranges we'd been given at a Welsh camp, their eyes widened and nearly popped out of their heads! No doubt it had been years since they'd even seen such a treasure. At other places we handed out chocolate bars and coloring books to children. It was great to see those precious faces glow with joy rather than fear—for a little while, anyway.

I recall seeing airplanes and small airstrips all over England and Wales. Rather than concentrating their airpower at a few large sites, the Allies wisely spread it out, making it more difficult for the Germans to locate and destroy aircraft. Allied air superiority would be key to winning the war.

Soon my outfit was ordered to go to the port of Southampton for the trip across the English Channel. Many of our guys had already left for Normandy as an advance group, arriving just two weeks after D-Day. Now it was my turn to hit the beaches, one month after the biggest military invasion in modern history. The sky at the port was filled with "Barrage Balloons." These were hydrogen-filled dirigibles that defended cities and harbors from Nazi aircraft. They were sixty-two feet long and twenty-five feet in diameter. Metal cables hung down from the balloons and sheared off the wings and propellers of low-flying planes trying to strafe us. The balloons were really effective against the German "Buzz Bomb" or the V1, an unmanned, guided missile that flew at just two thousand feet. More than one hundred V1s were claimed to have been destroyed using the "Barrages." The balloons also worked by forcing dive bombers to fly higher, well in range of our anti-aircraft weapons.

It took nearly all day to load our vehicles into the hold of the ship. Then we men walked the gang plank, loaded down with our weapons, barracks bags and gas masks. Once settled, we looked forward to that now-familiar rumble of the ship's engines coming alive. We would not feel her stir until early the next morning.

While waiting, excited yet a bit fearful, I reached into my jacket pocket and slipped out a small copy of the New Testament I kept pressed right against my heart. Behind its soft, warm, brown leather cover, lay the words that would encourage me now and throughout a lifetime:

"Do not be anxious about anything, but in everything, by prayer and petition, with thanksgiving, present your requests to God. And the peace of God, which transcends all understanding, will guard your hearts and minds in Christ Jesus"
(Philippians 4:6&7).

BAIE DE LA SEINE

Vau...
Etre...
C.d'Heu...
St Jour...

Cauvill...

Octeville

C.de la Heve
Sste Adress...

LE HAV...

...eur
...t-la Hougue
...le

Grand Camp les Bains
St Pierre du Mont
Isierville
St Laurent-s-M.
Ste Honorine des Pertes
Port en Bessin
Arromanches les Bains
Asnelles la Belle Plage
Courseulles-s-M.
St Aubin-s-M.
Langrune-s-M.
Luc-s-M.
Lion s-M.
Riva Bella

Villervi...
Trouville
Deauville
Villers-s-M.
Houlgate
le Home
Cabourg
Dozul...

la Cambe
Creully
Ouistreham
Isigny
BAYEUX
CAEN

Chapter Six

On y va! Our destination: "Bloody Omaha," one of the principal landing points on the beaches of Normandy. This area, about three-and-a-half miles long, ran from Sainte-Honorine-des-Pertes to Vierville-sur-Mer. Though its military codename was Omaha Beach, the nickname described its reputation as a killing field where over three thousand men were dead, wounded, or missing by the time evening fell on D-Day, June 6, 1944. Despite the horrific losses, thirty-four thousand soldiers did land safely. Then, through sheer guts and determination, they managed to climb the bluffs, organize themselves into small groups that spread across the plateau, attack the enemy from the rear, and declare victory. Though the beach was strewn with burning vehicles and the bodies of our courageous boys, the coastal villages were in Allied hands by nightfall. By July 1, the beachhead would be secure up to seventy miles along the coast and would welcome one million Allied troops and nearly two hundred thousand vehicles.

As we approached, one month later, we were more than ready to begin *our* work in France. It seemed to take forever for the big cranes to lift the vehicles from the ship and place them onto the landing crafts. My jeep and another were the last two to be dragged up from the hold. Finally, it was our turn to climb over the side of the ship and down the cargo net to enter the landing craft. This was no small challenge, since we carried those heavy barracks bags and weapons on our shoulders while we scrambled down the net. It was tough to hold on as the net thrashed back and forth in the wind. We really had to be careful at the bottom, so we weren't crushed between the two bouncing ships being slammed together by the waves.

As we headed toward shore, I realized how late it was in the day. The tide was going out, so the landing craft couldn't even get us to shore. The craft was forced to drive off into deeper water, and we had to try to drive the jeeps in on our own, in three feet of water. The jeeps that had gone in two weeks before us were specially water-proofed for just such an event, but ours weren't. Several of them conked out in the swirling waters and eventually had to be shoved on shore by bulldozers. As if this weren't fun enough, a lone, low-flying German plane swooped over us ominously but fired no shots.

We found ourselves finally on shore—alone. The rest of the 92nd Signal Battalion had gone on without us. Daylight was fading fast when a lieutenant with our small group encouraged us to bivouac or encamp under some trees. We pitched our pup-tents, four-by-four-foot pieces of canvas, and tried to catch a few winks in between taking turns standing guard over each other. We felt relatively safe, knowing that the beachhead was secure up to about fifteen miles inland, but still, we were on edge. All seemed fine, for most of the night, until we heard some rustling in the brush nearby. We were startled awake and quickly groped across the sand for our weapons, only to find ourselves nose-to-nose with a big old cow shoving her head through the dense branches, no doubt checking out her camp mates.

The next morning we set out to join the rest of our outfit, which we discovered camping in a field near Barneville-sur-Mer, just south of the beachhead. The days were quiet here, except for the constant whine of vehicles carrying men and supplies along the roads. The nights were a different story. Those same roads were under attack by German bombers ("Bed Check Charlie," to us), who tried to destroy them in order to stop us or, at the very least, slow us down. Our Corps rear had the scare of their lives one night when one of those bombers, a Stuka, was shot down by our anti-aircraft guns and then crashed and burned right in the middle of their tents. Amazingly, no one was killed, other than the unfortunate pilot. We had our own scare one day when suddenly a machine gun was spraying bullets everywhere as we sat around camp, only to discover that a jeep driver had been cleaning his gun with a loaded clip in it! Once again, praise God, no one was hurt.

A bright spot in the long days in Normandy was the daily visit by a little French girl, Yvette. A tall, slim child of twelve years, she came offering fresh green beans to the soldiers. She lived in Barneville with her mother. Her father, a French officer, was a prisoner of war. To this day, I have a heart for kids and want them to know Jesus as their Savior. This sweet child was no exception, so I took time to share Bible stories with her. I met Yvette's mom and, with her permission, I had my mom send some clothes and shoes to Yvette with money I'd sent to the States. Everything fit perfectly, and Yvette was thrilled. Knowing a little English, she wrote a nice thank you note to my mom and continued to write me for several months after our unit had moved on. In one letter, I was so relieved to hear that her father had been released and was safe at home. Yvette's letters, full of a child's boundless hope, were an encouragement to me in the midst of the horrors of war; I've kept her precious notes these many years.

We soldiers had visits by other children in the town who'd look up at us with their warm, dark eyes and implore, "*Avez-vous de chocolat ou de bonbon?*" My favorite was when they'd ask for "cow goommy." They had never seen nor tasted chewing gum before and obviously thought we looked like cows working on some cud! Though we had been given "invasion money," special bills and coins to be used during the war for food or extras, we often simply exchanged food with the townsfolk. We'd give them our Army rations, and they'd provide delicious dark bread and sour cream butter. I think we got the better end of the deal, *n'est-ce pas?*

The advance group from Companies A and B (we were the XV Corps of Patton's 3rd Army), which had arrived two weeks before us, was busy laying telephone and teletype wire from Corps headquarters to Division headquarters command posts. These "jump teams" were crucial in ensuring communication with the front lines. The problem was that these wires were often tapped by the enemy, allowing them to intercept vital intelligence. Also, the lines were often damaged in skirmishes and had to be repaired by the guys of Company C. My job was to provide another means of communication: sealed, coded messages, which I hand-delivered to the various

Army outfits throughout France. The messages were labeled either *priority*, *urgent*, or *rush*, and if stopped by the Nazis, we were instructed to first destroy all the messages, then destroy the jeep with a phosphorus grenade, and then run like the dickens (or "the devil")!

Message centers, which were located near Corps Headquarters in a thirty foot trailer pulled by a semi-tractor, held a big map inside. The map pointed out where the various divisions were supposed to be. The divisions' exact locations could be confusing, since their positions changed frequently, as did the maps we were provided. The generals and staff officers made their plans, wrote messages, had them encoded by men cleared by the FBI and ordered us to deliver them. Armed with the messages, fresh maps and my machine gun, I'd set out in my jeep to find the divisions and deliver the precious cargo. This proved more difficult than you'd imagine! I drove day and night on unfamiliar roads, covering hundreds of miles, often with very little sleep. Some days I drove for eighteen or twenty hours straight. As soon as I arrived at one location, I had to pick up more messages destined for the Infantry, Cavalry, Engineer or Armored divisions and, sleepily, set out again. On occasion, I'd take off my shoes and slacks, scoot into my sleeping bag and try to lie down under a shady tree near the center to get a little rest, only to be nudged awake all too soon and sent on my way to deliver more messages.

Simply navigating the roads was another challenge. In Normandy, I had to weave in and out of the nearly constant stream of convoys, which was nerve-wracking to say the least. I often found myself driving on the opposite side of the road (at least they drove on the "right" side of the road in France). One day I had several messages to deliver and was in a hurry, as always, when I came up behind a slow-going jeep containing its driver and an officer. I poured on the gas in order to pass him and was happily zipping down the left side of the road when I hit a huge shell hole in the pavement. The jeep flew into a ditch and landed in a culvert. The poor GI who rode with me soared over the windshield, skidded across the road, and sustained bad cuts and bruises. Just as in Ireland, my knees slammed into the dashboard so hard that I couldn't move, and the steering wheel punched me in the stomach. The driver of the jeep I'd passed stopped to help. I sheepishly handed over my messages to the officer on board for safe delivery. An ambulance took us to a field hospital where we were cared for and even offered Purple Hearts! We, of course, had to refuse them, since we were injured by my own actions, not those of our adversaries. (However, the enemy was most likely to blame for that crater in the road!)

Driving at night was the biggest challenge of all, especially with no lights, as you'll recall. We had to worry about getting lost and possibly ending up in enemy territory, critters on the road, snipers in the woods, bombers overhead, and the most frightening possibility: piano wire. During the day, we usually drove with the windshield down. This helped us to see better, despite the bugs that would slap us in the face! But at night, the Germans would string piano wire across the roads at precisely the right level to break a neck or slice off a head as you zoomed by. I drove in the dark with the windshield tipped up to deflect any wire, while some drivers retrofitted their vehicles with a tall metal bar fastened to the front bumper which would catch the wire before it could decapitate anyone. I'm very thankful to the Lord that I still have my head on straight!

Chapter Seven

Les Bocages. It was time for us to move out of the camp at Barneville and into the hedgerows or *bocages* further west. These thick tangles of oak, elm and beech trees, shrubs, and vines were grown on tall mounds of soil to act as fences around the farmers' fields and livestock. They stood more than ten feet tall and were several feet thick, often with a narrow channel in the center where one could move freely. The Germans had already discovered them as excellent defensive positions, where they could hide their tanks, snipe our men and launch their anti-tank weapons undetected. The hedgerows were not favorable to the offensive warfare for which our guys were trained. Though it usually took three Americans to rout one "Kraut," successful fighting amid the hedgerows required five of our men. We suffered many more casualties than expected until someone had a brilliant idea. A master sergeant named Cullen salvaged these huge, iron "teeth," which the Germans had sunk in the sand of the beaches to swamp our incoming tanks and vehicles. These teeth were then welded to the front of our Sherman tanks and were capable of ripping through the hedgerows and destroying the enemy's secret lairs. This new-found vehicle, called a "Rhino," also let us cross the fields with relative ease and forced the Germans to rely on the very roads they insisted on bombing.

One of the intact hedgerows kept me alive, however. I dug a foxhole onto the side of one and covered half the hole with my pup-tent. It was so nice to crawl into my den and feel safe at the end of a day spent dodging vehicles and bombs while on the roads. One evening, as an entire U.S. tank outfit in the next field was started up and ready to move out, about fifteen Nazi planes thundered overhead and flew toward the ocean about ten miles away. Suddenly, they made a U-turn and headed straight back toward our position. The planes spread out, dropped low and began strafing everything in sight. Several trucks exploded, sending up radiant, red flames and thick, black smoke. Other trucks with mounted machine guns returned fire, igniting a chorus of shots from all over the field. I dove through a hole I had torn into a hedgerow and scrunched down as far as possible, thankful for a big mound of dirt that protected me. The bullets pummeled the ground, making an occasional pinging sound as they ricocheted off rocks.

After it had quieted a bit, I peered out only to see one plane right over me. It was smoking badly and the pilot was so close I could clearly see him frantically looking around. I aimed my machine gun toward him but felt no need to shoot. His plane just kept sputtering and losing altitude, and then quickly disappeared. The remaining planes took off as well, leaving us a chance to catch our breath and calm our pounding chests. The old saying about there being no atheists in foxholes (or hedgerows) sure must be true! Later, we heard that that air raid was part of an effort by the Germans to push through our line and cut us in half. Since we controlled the skies during the day, allowing supply convoys on the ground to pick up and deliver fuel, food and ammunition, the enemy conducted nighttime air raids to do as much damage as possible to roads and bridges. Our Army Air Force responded by converting P38s into night fighters. They were painted black and given the best radar available at the time in order to detect Nazi aircraft.

I encountered the Nazi planes another night. As I drove out of the mountain city of Avranches, a huge flare lit up directly over me, which had been dropped by parachute from a German plane and made the black sky as bright as day for about a half mile. Its job was to act as a giant spotlight, lighting the way for their bombers. The flare's brilliance forced a buddy and me to abruptly pull off the road and to hide the jeep under a tree. I dove into a hedgerow, but my pal disappeared. Soon, dozens of red and green flares began sizzling around me. I knew I wasn't alone, though, as I heard a machine gun being fired nearby. I could see the red glow of the tracer bullets, every fifth bullet shot, as an attempt was made to bring down the flares. But they had already done their deed. The bombers quickly followed fast and furious. Their screaming shells slammed relentlessly into the earth, making the ground shudder and the dirt hammer my body. I grabbed my head in my hands and held it down tightly as I prayed for God's mercy.

As suddenly as it had begun, it was over. Darkness and a cautious quiet returned. I yelled for my friend as I shook off a coat of soil. There was nothing but silence. After several minutes, I finally heard his muffled cry. I followed the sound and unearthed Marvin, a fellow Christian from Texas, lying on the side of the road with his big, old head stuck in a culvert and a heavy pile of dirt covering his legs. Now if he had just used that head, he would have joined me in the hedgerow instead of being a sitting duck at the side of the road! Once again, God heard our prayers and delivered us both.

Despite the narrow escape, we had to get to Corps rear to receive more mail and messages and return to...Avranches! The MP ordered us to take a different route back, which took us near the seashore and then up into the mountains. Another MP, hiding in the shadows at the edge of a seaside town, warned us of a sniper ahead. The full moon that night would light our way, but would also make us easy targets for the German paratroopers who had infiltrated the mountains. They delighted in picking off the lead driver of the convoys, forcing the entire group to stop cold and then scramble to regroup. They would surely delight in nailing me, too!

My partner and I crammed our bodies as low as possible in the jeep and placed the heavy mail bags behind us like a wall. I floored the pedal, pushing that jeep to the max, and began our climb up the heavily tree-lined road. The long shadows of those trees were our only refuge from the snipers who took pot shots at us every time the jeep slipped from shadow to moonlight and back again. It seemed we were ahead in this game of cat-and-mouse until I hit a huge hole in the pavement, lost control and nearly careened down the mountainside. Somehow, I regained control and continued to speed along the road toward Avranches, holding my breath as we ducked in and out of the shadows. We finally arrived in one piece. I felt cold trickles of sweat run down my forehead as I gave myself permission to breathe again. We were very glad that the bridge to Avranches was still intact and that the Allied anti-aircraft guns were positioned and ready for defense. We delivered our "wall" of messages and headed back to camp by yet another route. I was so grateful to be able to crawl into my foxhole and fall dead asleep that night.

After we broke through at Avranches, Patton's 3rd Army began to close a large gap between the British Army and ours. The Brits were pushing south toward Falaise while the Americans pushed north, creating a pocket of Germans stuck in the middle. Sixty thousand enemy troops were caught or killed as we advanced, but thousands more escaped somehow along a road clogged with horses, wagons, tanks and trucks, and then streamed southeast toward Paris.

In the midst of all this, my buddy and I were trying to deliver messages. We decided to team up with another pair of messengers one night—four in a jeep seemed safer, somehow. German soldiers had scattered at the Avranches breakthrough so you never knew when or where you might confront one. It was so dark and creepy that night that I slid the jeep into low gear and then crawled through a deep, black forest. While trying my best to remain on the seemingly invisible road, I glanced from side-to-side for any signs of the enemy shrouded by massive tree trunks and heavy branches. Having driven all night, we were greatly relieved to emerge from the forest at daybreak and see that we were near our destination: the 2nd French Armored Division's message center. While approaching, we heard French tanks rumbling as they were aligned behind the hedgerows in a square box formation with their guns pointing outward to protect the center. We quickly delivered our messages and began to leave when we saw American planes swooping down into the forest we'd just exited and blasting the living daylights out of the trees. We attempted to leave the area by another road only to be stopped abruptly by French soldiers who exclaimed, "*La Boche! La Boche!*" (meaning "blockhead"), while pointing down the road to where some Germans had been spotted, no doubt lying in wait. As we backed up and sped away in yet another direction, I felt we were not alone—God was working overtime to keep us safe.

Daylight exposed the many victims of war. The beautiful countryside was littered with blackened, mangled vehicles and tanks. Dead cows were lying on their backs across the deep green fields, their bodies puffed up like giant balloons. Hugely swollen udder bags shoved the cows' legs apart as their bloated bellies rose toward the sky. On occasion, a soldier would shoot one, releasing foul-smelling gas. Believe me, they smelled bad enough without being ripped open by a bullet. German tanks holding their dead boys stank even worse as the hot July sun beat down on their metal coffins. I was forced to shove my nose inside my field jacket as I drove by. I held my breath as long as possible, and then just gagged uncontrollably when I was forced to inhale the putrid air.

I remember looking down from my jeep to see a well-dressed Frenchman lying along the road. The contents of his suitcase were scattered beside his motionless body. No doubt he'd made a futile attempt toward safety. The Normandy area had been devastated by the Germans. Over ten thousand people had lost their lives in that region alone. The French soldiers would take a measure of revenge, however, on the Nazi prisoners of war as they marched them down the dusty roads. The captives were badly treated by the French, who would first dig through their pockets and wallets, removing anything of value. Next, they'd hurl photos of loved ones onto the ground and mash them into the soil with their boots. The prisoners were shoved around, slapped and beaten with abandon. I don't know what happened to them after that, but I witnessed many hundreds being herded across the country.

Any French women suspected of fraternizing with the Germans and/or collaborating with them weren't treated very well by their compatriots, either. In some of the towns, I saw women who had had all their hair cut off as punishment for having been seen with German soldiers. There were rumors of women being severely beaten or "tarred and feathered," or even shot for the same offense.

Such treatment was nothing, though, compared to the atrocities committed by the Waffen-SS against French civilians in countless occupied towns and villages. The SS was the dreaded German special security force, which also ran the concentration camps under Heinrich Himmler. (Himmler would be responsible for more deaths than any other man who ever lived, aside from Hitler and Stalin.) Those suspected of harming German soldiers or of being a member of one of the French Resistance groups (such as the rural Maquis) were systematically rounded up, tortured, and slaughtered in unspeakable ways I can't bring myself to describe. Their brutal murders contributed to the estimated 270,000 civilian deaths in France alone, during the long years of war.

Chapter Eight

Bon appétit! There was more to Army life than just dodging Stukas and snipers. There was *la nourriture, la hygiène, et les femmes!* My buddies and I often stopped by local farms and asked for fresh food to supplement our Army rations. The farmers would gladly bring out eggs wrapped in brown paper, dark bread and sour cream butter. We gave them some of our canned goods containing beef stew, beans or vegetable hash. Again, their kids were thrilled with the huge chocolate bars and gum we shared. We also had large cans of bacon that we fried up, and then we cooked the eggs in the heavy grease. Fried eggs and bacon were so delicious with that French bread and butter. One time, our buck sergeant, who was a driver also, caught a bunch of chickens running down the road. I'll never forget the great fried chicken dinner we devoured that night.

When we had to resort to canned food, a nifty way to heat it was to mold a burner from a metal biscuit can, fill it with gasoline, and light her up. The jeep's engine also served as a nice oven while we were on the road. We'd place a can of hash or stew on the manifold, then stop from time to time to see how swollen the can was. When it seemed just right, we'd punch a hole in the can to release the steam and then dig in. Sometimes we were too late, and we'd find that our dinner had exploded and was baked onto the engine. If all else failed, a blow torch worked well to heat a meal quickly.

The water the Army provided was terrible. A big, canvas, rubber-lined bag filled with water and heaven-knows-how-many chemicals was hung from a tree in the hot sun. It was like drinking a bubbling potion from a chemistry lab! I couldn't stand it; so disregarding the Army rules warning us not to drink the local water, I filled up my canteen with cool, refreshing water from farm wells. It must have been fine, because I never got sick on it. I had two canteens: one to share with the guys, who kept asking me for a swig, and one reserved just for me. (I wasn't being selfish—it's just that they smoked and drank a lot, and I didn't want the residue to spoil the fresh water.)

Beverages enjoyed by my buddies such as wine, schnapps, and Calvados were made with the tart fruit of the many apple trees in that area. Calvados, a really strong apple brandy, was in such abundance that people simply gave it away, much to my friends' delight. They didn't always take it in moderation, though. One day a lieutenant, who was usually a nice guy, and his buddy had been enjoying a bit too much of the drink when they asked me to drive them to the showers. I agreed, and while traveling along, the lieutenant suddenly ordered me to stop beside a Frenchman who was walking down the road. The lieutenant grabbed his rifle and jabbed it toward the man, with his finger poised on the trigger. The poor man was terrified, raised his hands up shakily and pleaded for his life in a flurry of French. The lieutenant just laughed and mocked me when I told him to knock it off. I was so angry and ashamed of him that I thought of arresting the jerk myself. However, the lieutenant quit the torment on his own, and we continued on our way. I dropped the pair off at the showers and refused to drive them any longer, indeed, ever again. I'll bet it took a long time for that Frenchman to get over it—as if there wasn't enough terror around.

Hygiene in the battlefield was interesting. You quickly learned to be creative with your helmet. It became a cooking pot, a wash basin and a laundromat! We used it as a sink to wash ourselves and our clothes. We sometimes filled our helmets with gasoline and dipped our clothes in it, much like dry cleaning. It worked pretty well, if you didn't mind smelling like a gas station for a few days. White areas, like inside pockets, turned pink, but that faded after awhile also. When sponge-bathing out of the helmet wasn't doing the trick, we'd hop into the nearest river to clean up. One day while we were bathing, some local women came out to do their laundry in the same stream. Big smiles broke out on their faces as they encountered a bunch of naked GIs. It was embarrassing to say the least. We were really lucky when we found the Quartermaster outfit. They'd set up showers at streams and heat the water for us—and provide lots of soap and clean towels. We'd feel like a million bucks after a hot shower!

We learned not only to be chefs and launderers but barbers as well. Although a real barber would go around and offer to cut your hair for fifty cents, we men who were always on the road never ran across him. So we did the best we could giving each other a haircut with a small pair of scissors and a comb. We didn't think we looked too bad!

Finding somewhere to sleep for the night was often interesting. Some nights while in the woods, we'd park several jeeps around us like a box. We'd lie on the ground in the middle of the vehicles, so we wouldn't worry about passing trucks running us over as we snoozed. Other nights, I'd scrounge around for some hay and make a fluffy bed on the ground. We also tried to find abandoned buildings to sleep in. One night, four of us found one bed in an old factory. We laid on it crosswise with rickety chairs to hold up our feet. We slept like rocks until sometime near dawn when I began to sense we weren't alone. I switched on my flashlight only to see thousands of bedbugs swarming across the rotting wall above my head. Some brave bugs were leaping off the wall and onto that pathetic bed, like tiny paratroopers, in order to enjoy an early breakfast on us: literally. We all hopped up and began to swat at the little devils in the pale morning light. One guy grabbed a blow torch, filled it with gasoline and incinerated as many bugs as he could find. They were toast—so was the bed!

One fond memory was seeing Bing Crosby, Bob Hope, and Dinah Shore during a USO show, when thousands of GIs were entertained in a huge, bombed-out factory. We roared at their jokes and skits and swooned at their songs. The guys really showed their appreciation for the pretty girls singing and dancing on stage, although it was hard to hear with all those men whooping it up! At one point, one of the girls picked a GI out of the audience, invited him on stage, put her arms around him and sang him a love song. She ended by giving him a great big kiss before sending him back to his seat. The crowd went wild, whistling and yelling.

Every soldier wished he had been that lucky guy. It was nice to take our minds off reality, for at least a little while.

Another highlight was my one and only break since I'd left New York over eight months ago, and the only break I'd get during the entire war! That time was spent in none other than Paris, though getting there was tricky. As we neared the River Seine, we set up camp in a wooded area on a hill. Standing at the edge of the woods, you could look across the river and watch our shells exploding on the opposite bank, very near the front lines. One-hundred-fifty millimeter Long Toms and Howitzers were being launched from down in a nearby hollow. The shells flew right over our heads by the hundreds. The trees, the tents, and our clothes shook violently from the wind created as the ammo whooshed by on its way to the targets. You could see a little spotter plane flying over the river, pointing out where our guys should aim the artillery. I was thankful not to have that job. It wasn't much safer in the woods, though, as German fighter planes frequently strafed the area. The sound of their engines groaning overhead forced me to jump helplessly behind the nearest tree. A barrage of bullets penetrated the thick branches. My guardian angel must have joined me there as I was miraculously spared any hot metal searing or piercing my flesh.

Things got really hairy when I had to cross pontoon bridges spanning the Seine, in order to deliver messages. Large smoke pots perched all around belched billowing gray clouds. This smoke screen covered an area about two hundred feet high and three or four blocks wide, to hide the temporary structures from German bombers. Unfortunately, the smoke also made it difficult to see very far ahead while crossing, so you had to pray that no one else was coming from the opposite way!

I faced an even more challenging obstacle one morning while trying to cross a pontoon bridge. Although I knew motor messengers had top priority on the roads, before tanks or other vehicles, apparently no one had informed the major who was directing traffic at the entrance. He insisted on standing in front of my jeep to stop me from proceeding and to allow his tanks access. I put the jeep in low gear and slowly moved forward, pushing him until he was forced to spring aside. His face turned a blotchy red color and he ran up to me sputtering a demand for my name. I told him I'd give my name after hearing his and then threatened to turn him in to Corps Headquarters. Despite waving the envelopes labeled "urgent" in his face, the major ordered me to stay put. I took off anyway and began to dart in and out between the tanks churning across the bridge. After a successful delivery on the other side, I returned to the message center and learned that everyone was talking about how I'd stood up to a guy who was ten years older and a foot taller than me! I may have seemed brave or even crazy, but I was simply obeying my superior's orders and following the rules.

We all had to take our turn at guard duty at the camp. One night, after putting in my mandated two hours, I anxiously waited for my replacement to arrive. I ended up standing guard, literally, all night long, because no one ever came to relieve me. Despite my burning legs and chalk-dry mouth, the thought of being court-martialed and possibly shot for abandoning my post kept me on my feet until early morning, when someone finally arrived. The only good thing was that, though they offered no explanation or apology, when my superiors heard about this, they dismissed me from performing guard duty until after the war ended.

We broke camp and continued eastward until just past Paris. Our messages were few at this point, so we were detached by the Corps and given that break. Ignoring an order to stay out of Paris, my buddies and I disconnected the odometers on our jeeps and headed back to the City of Light. (What red-blooded GI could resist?) Paris had been liberated just three days earlier on August 25, 1944 after four years of German occupation, so you can imagine the evidence of joy, relief and excitement that met us as we entered the city. My buddies and I were amazed to see hundreds of thousands of people still lined up along *la Champs Elysées* waving, smiling and cheering wildly. We drove right up to *l'Arc de Triomphe,* then parked our vehicles and began to stroll around to join the exuberant crowd and to see the sights.

I traded several candy bars with someone for a guidebook to the Parisian landmarks. We walked under *la Tour Eiffel*, in awe of its size and beauty, and marveled at *le Cathédrale de Notre-Dame* and *le Sacré Coeur.* Paris had declared itself an "open city," which meant it had abandoned any defensive efforts, allowing the Germans to march in with little resistance. This was an effort to preserve lives and landmarks, and it worked pretty well—until the Normandy Invasion. As Hitler observed the Allied advance toward Paris, he ordered his garrison commander, Dietrich von Choltitz, to burn the city. The Germans began rigging the main bridges across the Seine with explosives, then started on plans for the monuments: *la Tour Eiffel, bien sur,* would be the first to go. Thankfully, due to personal and political considerations, Choltitz had a last-minute change of heart and refused to obey the order to leave Paris a smoking

ruin. Knowing all this, we had a special appreciation for being able to see the Parisians alive and ecstatic now and to visit first-hand places we'd only seen in a picture postcard.

My photograph was taken in a small studio in Paris. I was feeling pretty smug when told that I was the first American soldier to have been photographed there—until the other GIs swaggered in. They stood there all flushed with excitement as they boasted about being surrounded by beautiful French women, nearly smothered with hugs and kisses, then given gifts of wine and tomatoes! Not being one to miss out on affection from a young lady, I made up for it later as we filled our jeep with *jolies filles*, hugging and kissing us as we drove them around town. (Smart me, I fought to sit in the back of the jeep rather than drive that day!) Times like that sure helped encourage us as we said "*à tout à l'heure*" to Paris and began the agonizing final push across eastern France and into Germany.

Chapter Nine

Enfin... Fénétrange. The next stop was Lunéville, in the Alsace-Lorraine region of France, near the German border. Members of the HQ and HQ Company were housed there in a grand chateau beside a river. We ambled down a long bridge that took us to the front of the chateau. A huge door opened through which we drove our jeeps and parked within the relative safety of the thick walls surrounding the estate. On the first floor (the second level to we Americans), we tossed our sleeping bags on the marble floor and tried to make ourselves comfortable. It was short-lived, though, as German shells could be heard exploding quite close to the chateau. No sirens ever alerted us to attacks in the towns, so the sound of the German 88s themselves was our only warning. We scrambled to drag our beds down to the main floor, sleeping more confidently next to our jeeps behind those heavy walls. Somehow, we slept right through all the racket—guess we'd had months to practice.

The next morning I began a message run by

driving back over the long bridge and turning left onto the main street. I'd traveled only a block or two when I heard more shells screaming by and blowing up behind me. As much as my heart told me to go back and see what had happened, my mind told me I needed to complete my assignment. Hand delivery of messages by our 92nd Signal Battalion was more crucial than ever as Patton's 3rd Army advanced rapidly toward the German border. I forced myself to continue speeding out of town to finish my job, saying a quick prayer for the troops and civilians who may have been victims of the blasts.

Later that day, someone at the message center asked whether I'd heard about what happened at Lunéville: Hitler's barbarians had targeted civilians on the bridge, the same one I had crossed that morning. Several men from HQ and HQ were able to help with the recovery. They said the scene was awful, of course, just awful—all those people crying, wounded and dead, especially the children, all along the expanse of the bridge. Standing in stunned disbelief, I thought back to the many residents I'd passed that morning on the bridge: old men taking a leisurely stroll with their berets pulled over their eyes a bit to protect them from the glare of the early sun, a newspaper tucked under one arm, and a pipe tucked in their mouths; women returning from the market with a basket full of late-summer produce, bought with the few francs they had left in the world; and young children heading to the village schoolhouse, freshly scrubbed and dressed in worn but clean cotton uniforms. The children would gleefully chase each other as they made their way across, stopping here and there to toss a few crumbs from their morning *baguette* to the squawking ducks gathering in the river below.

I imagined their shrieks of delight turning to shrieks of terror as they began to realize what was happening and to run wildly through the choking black smoke, desperate to escape the assault. The Nazi cowards would run off deep into the woods, so pleased with themselves, so pleased with the carnage. I ran out of the message center and dropped to my knees, praying with all my might for those innocent souls whose everyday lives and bodies were suddenly, mercilessly, ripped apart by the shrapnel of an enemy who knew no shame.

With heavy hearts, we had to press on, moving into the area of Sarrebourg, France in the Vosges Mountains. It was now early autumn and the weather was getting cooler, especially at that higher elevation. We continued to scrounge around for any old buildings to stay in, such as barns, schools or barracks—anything to get out of the chilly night air. One town where we found shelter seemed secure enough, but after I'd left in the morning to deliver messages to nearby outfits, the town was shelled by a German railway gun. Those were enormous artillery pieces, as big as a battleship's, which ran on tracks and could shoot their ordnance toward targets up to thirty miles away. Entire buildings could be blown apart with just one shell.

When I dared go back to town, I hardly recognized it. Smoking piles of gray rubble sat where homes and shops once stood. Bodies wrapped in muslin sheets, some with brownish-red stains seeping through, were lined up in front of the office of the town *médecin*, his building being one of the few still intact. The townsfolk were weeping softly, wandering through the dusty haze. The message center was nowhere to be found. I was beginning to worry whether my buddies were lying somewhere beneath the mounds of stone and splintered wood, when I was told the center had been re-located to a large gravel pit about a mile away.

As I carefully drove there over a debris-covered road, I saw a jeep body dangling from a branch way up in a tree. It must have been hit by one of those shells, or maybe blown up by a land mine. I was surprised also to see a King Tiger, the biggest German tank ever, all 68 tons of it. Protected by 180mm of frontal armor and armed with an 88mm gun, it was a frightening thing to behold. I wasn't sure why it was abandoned there, but I could guess. I had heard that under the stress of the tank's massive size, its 700hp engine often overheated and died. It also was a gas hog, and fuel was getting harder and harder to come by, for both sides, as the winter months approached. In fact, General Eisenhower had decided to stop the advance on Germany for the winter, so we could regroup and replenish our supplies, especially gasoline. HQ and HQ Company, our hospital division, and Corps Headquarters were all pulled back thirty or forty miles and ordered to stay put. The war was sort of at a stalemate, so we would remain in one town for the next four months: Fénétrange.

Fénétrange was a picturesque village of stone cottages, a church, a few shops including a *charcuterie* and a *boulangerie*, and about three hundred folks who called it home. It was framed by dense green forests spreading across gently rolling hills. Our captain scouted out some places for us to stay. He found an extra bedroom for me and a guy named Vitale, in a weathered, three-bedroom house attached to an old chateau. The chateau overlooked a river in the back and was flanked by a garden, heavy with vegetables waiting to be plucked from withering vines on one side, and an animal pen, heavy with a fat pig on the other. Clumps of flowers, delphiniums I guess, were still soaking up the pale rays of October sun and decorating the lawn with their lavender-blue blossoms. Bees were buzzing, working furiously to drink in the last of the sweet flower nectar to make enough honey for their brood to last the winter.

Vitale, a nice-looking guy with shiny black hair thanks to his Italian-Jewish heritage, the captain, and I went to the back door of the house and headed up a staircase to our room on the upper floor, our boots making a heavy thud on each tread. The simple room held a double bed and a commode: a small bureau with doors below, covering a chamber pot. A blue-flowered basin and pitcher sat on the bureau and a hand-woven rug rested on the floor. A tiny window with a lacy white curtain overlooked the grassy yard below. It had been such a long time since I'd been in a real house, in a real bedroom. I immediately flopped down on the bed, passing my hand over the smooth, clean sheets and burrowing my head into the fluffy feather pillow. Lying on a real bed was absolute heaven, compared to the many months of trying to get comfortable in a hard, damp foxhole or on a scratchy pile of hay crawling with those cursed cooties! Now that I finally had a decent bed to enjoy for awhile, I'd have to recall my bed-making skills learned at Camp Crowder. (That time seemed an eternity ago.) I actually ended up just tossing my sleeping bag on top of the bedding so I wouldn't mess it up.

All too soon, the captain announced it was time to go downstairs to meet our new French hosts. Reluctantly, I rose and followed him and Vitale, feeling that I could have slept in that bed for a month without waking up! But what awaited me at the bottom of the stairs would prove to be better than a million wonderful nights of rest. Our eyes met instantly the second I entered the hallway. I hazily remember shaking hands with a large man and his petite wife as introductions were made, but my gaze never left the lavender-blue eyes of their young daughter, Delphine. I couldn't help noticing that those eyes were as bright a blue as those flowers outside. Suddenly, she was heartily shaking my hand and flashing a bright smile toward me. Thick waves of dark brown hair framed her delicate face and fell on slim shoulders. I sensed her hand in mine—hers felt small and cool while mine was hot, rough, damp and probably not too clean. She didn't seem to mind, though, and held my hand for what seemed like a blissfully long time.

Later in the week, I would meet Delphine's brother, Etienne. (By Providence, I believe, he would become a dear friend very late in life.) Delphine and her step-mother showered us with "*bonjour*" and "*bienvenu*," while her father stood nearby, silent and sullen. I figured that having American soldiers staying in his home wasn't exactly his idea. Or that he didn't speak much English. Or that he plain didn't like us for some reason. Or worse, he'd caught on that I was already mesmerized by his daughter. I would later learn that his cold attitude was due to all these things and more. Having greeted our hosts, we excused ourselves to get our barracks bags from the jeep and to haul them up to our new home.

Chapter Ten

Une rêve. A dream—that's what the next few months were like for me. I don't recall all of the details of my time in Fénétrange, being in a bit of a daze, but I'll never forget how I felt: on "cloud nine!" Each morning I do remember being up and out of the house very early to deliver messages. Within a minute of my return to the chateau late in the afternoon, she'd appear before me, like magic. Delphine's blue eyes would twinkle with delight and her cherry-red lips would move rapidly as she greeted me in French. She spoke English pretty well also, but would burst into her native language whenever she was excited.

Within a week of our meeting, those lovely lips were being put to even better use—smooching! We'd softly talk about our day, which would soon lead to some good kissing. And not just little pecks, mind you. I offered nice, firm, long kisses, which she gladly returned. It seemed she'd had a bit of practice already, by the age of nineteen. But so had I. My skills were honed at the tender age of fourteen or fifteen on the skating pond back in Minneapolis. I used to skate up next to a girl and hold an oak leaf over her head, pretending it was mistletoe, and would proceed to lock lips when she turned toward me (if I didn't get slapped first, which I never did)! The girls in the neighborhood and I also played "Post Office." I was given the enviable role of Postmaster and the girls would tell me how many "stamps" (or kisses) they'd like to purchase. Boy, could I deliver!

Anyway, I sure looked forward to getting my work done, then returning home to Delphine. I'd never had a true girlfriend before, so having her melt into my arms, smelling fresh and sweet like that good lavender soap they had in France, was heaven at the end of a long day. In the evening, she and I would spend time with her family playing card games or just talking in the warm kitchen, waiting for what seemed an eternity for her parents to go to bed so we could have some time alone. We'd often talk and kiss until 11:00 or 12:00, even though I had to get up very early. She'd slowly, reluctantly, walk me up the stairs to my room for a final goodnight kiss at my door. Then Delphine would tip-toe down the hall, through her parent's room and into her own adjoining one. I'd lie awake for a long while, just thinking about her and not quite believing my good fortune in having been kissed by an angel!

My roommate, Vitale, spent very little time at the chateau, so I had the whole bed to myself most nights. Vitale, being quite the ladies' man, usually spent the night with some dame in town. He thought he was so charming that once he even tried to steal a kiss from Delphine, right in front of me. He took her a bit too literally when she exclaimed that she "could just kiss him," after he had presented her with a small gift. She giggled and pushed him away, but the dirty look I gave him let him know beyond a doubt that she was off-limits. He kept his distance after that.

She had caught someone else's eye, too. One night I returned to the house late and was surprised to see a fellow GI from the 92nd standing alone in the kitchen. He was all spiffed up and smelling up the room with his cologne and hair tonic. His clean uniform, shiny hair, and polished boots made me suspect the worst: that he was there for a date with Delphine. I gave him a brief glance and nod as I passed by and headed up the stairs to wash. I returned to my room, leaving the door open a crack, not knowing whether to head back down or to just stay in my room and hope Delphine would come to me. I decided to wait there awhile. I could tell that Delphine and her step-mother were discussing something intensely in the bedroom next to me, but couldn't get a grip on what they were saying. Suddenly, the house was very quiet for a few minutes. Next, I heard footsteps on the stairs, muffled voices in the kitchen, and the wooden door leading outside bang shut. I sat quietly, waiting. My mind began to race. Had Delphine left with that guy? Was it her idea or, more likely, her parent's? Was I a chump for thinking that the last several weeks were as special for her as they had been for me? Was some little twerp going to be holding and kissing her at the end of the night instead of me?

I fought feelings of fear and anger welling up in me, knowing in my mind that they were plain silly at this point in our relationship, but those feelings still pushed me to scramble down the stairs to see what was going on. I practically burst into the kitchen, only to see Delphine and her step-mom calmly sitting at the old wooden table, preparing the evening meal and talking about getting ready for the quickly-approaching winter. At first, Delphine looked up at me with her bright smile but her expression quickly changed to curiosity and then to amusement as she read the panic on my face and guessed its cause. She later explained that the young man had just shown up at her door uninvited and was wondering whether she'd go with him to a local dance, as she had done a few times before. At first, her step-mother encouraged her to go, but when Delphine explained that she and I were interested in each other, her step-mother smiled knowingly and sent the poor sap on his way. I realized then that I had an ally in her.

On occasion I was able to get a pass to spend an entire day with Delphine. I didn't care what we did—just being with her was enough. I'd help her pick dandelion greens for salad or gather flowers to place on her mother's grave, resting in the small church courtyard nearby. She often visited the gravesite, which had a built-in stone vase for flowers and a picture frame cradling a photo of her mother. Though the image was quite faded, I could tell she had had the same dark hair and brilliant eyes that now drew me to her daughter. Her French mother had, sadly, passed away within days of giving birth to Etienne, Delphine's younger brother. Her aunt came to live with and care for the young family. Later, she married their father and so took on the role of step-mother as well as aunt. Delphine and her brother now called Genevieve, their step-mom, simply "*maman*," since she was the only one they'd ever really known. Delphine didn't remember much about her mother, being just a two-year-old when she died, but she lovingly honored her each week with a visit and fresh flowers.

Once in a while, we would do something relaxing, such as taking a ride in a French duck boat. The boat reminded me of a two-man kayak that sat low in the water and was propelled by two paddles. The little river right behind the chateau was the perfect place to launch her. The river meandered past the chateau, through the town and out into the countryside. We'd quietly glide by cows munching the last of autumn's bright green grass, unaware of the splendid setting that was their dining room. Elegant white swans would slip alongside the boat and then overtake it with their own powerful paddles. Although delighting in the scenery, I kept my eyes on Delphine sitting in front of me, as she'd turn her head to flash me that smile or giggle as she'd playfully splash me a bit. We made a pretty good team, paddling in unison and maneuvering the waterway, which got me to thinking we'd be a pretty good team on land, too!

That river was also known for fishing. One day, Delphine's brother ran up to the house shouting with joy as he showed off his haul: an enormous carp. The wonderful smell of fish baking in the oven that afternoon wafted up to my room and made my stomach growl out loud. To my surprise and delight, Vitale and I were invited to eat the fish with the family. This was a big occasion. They even had the meal in the best room of the house, the dining room, rather than in the kitchen as usual. Now most folks back in Minnesota, the land of 11,842 lakes, wouldn't think of eating a bottom-feeder like carp, since walleye and trout are abundant there. But you can't imagine how delicious that fish was after months and months of eating Army rations that tasted about as good as the boxes or cans in which they came!

We really enjoyed our time with the family that evening, too. Delphine's mom was always pleasant enough, but her father often sat gloomily, giving me mean glances from time to time—until tonight. Suddenly, he grew more animated as he struck up a conversation with Vitale—in German. Vitale spoke not only Italian and French, but some German as well. Then it dawned on me: Delphine's father was a "Kraut!" Many people just like him in those cities bordering France and Germany must have felt a divided allegiance to their homeland and their adopted country. My own dad, who had been born in Germany but raised in America, may have faced that dilemma, but his loyalty was always to the United States. (I used to tease my Army buddies that it was a good thing he emigrated to Minnesota, or else I would have ended up fighting on the German side, and Hitler would have won the war!) Anyway, learning that her dad was German would help me understand some things later on.

The Germans, and French for that matter, love their drink. Delphine's dad was no exception and made his very own wine, schnapps, and Calvados in his still. A big metal barrel filled with old, brown, mushy apples sat in the corner of a shed. The fruit would sit there for months until adequately fermented. A fire was set under the barrel and soon steam would rise and pass through a long, curved pipe where it would cool, condense and drip out into a bottle as alcohol. I'm not sure what the proof level was of that home-brew, but it smelled something like apple-scented paint thinner as it bubbled away!

Her dad also raised *un grand cochon* in a small pen next to the house. As the days grew shorter and colder, it was time to butcher the plump hog. The chilly weather would help preserve some of the fresh pork, and the rest would be smoked so there would be meat all winter. The wonderful aroma of smoking hams, hocks, and sides of bacon filled the yard and house for days. Root vegetables, which had been mulched with leaves and pine needles, were also pulled up from the cold, stiff ground after a hard frost and placed in a root cellar dug into the earth below the shed. Potatoes, carrots, and turnips could be safely stored for months underground in the zero-degree Celsius "refrigerator," as could the cured meat, canned fruits and vegetables, and even dairy products. By God's grace, those provisions would sustain the family through the winter months and through whatever turmoil the war and its aftermath could yet create.

Chapter Eleven

Wintertide. Icy winds began to blow a thin layer of newly-fallen snow into eddies. The small whirlpools churned in circles, paused briefly, then gathered speed and continued to dust the roads and fields with white. The snow built up quickly and soon was as high as the hood of my jeep. One time I had to bust my way through a snowdrift by flooring the jeep over and over until I'd forged an opening through the frozen wall. We also had no antifreeze in those days, so every night we had to remember to drain our radiators and fill them up with water from farm wells each morning.

Though not quite as cold as Minnesota in December, the mountain air, nevertheless, would pierce right through your clothes and heavy coat. We had been issued only one pair each of thin, leather gloves and boots. Our hands and feet would nearly freeze as we drove the open jeep through the Vosges Mountains. I was grateful that later, in Strasbourg, France, I was able to visit a large warehouse filled with German goods. The warehouse had been abandoned by the Germans as the assault against France's occupiers intensified. I was allowed to take some knives and forks engraved with the Nazi eagle and swastika symbols, a blanket, some canteens, German soldier pants, a jacket and a belt buckle. My buddies got a kick out of me putting on the uniform and parading around; I looked just like a Kraut officer! I also found a bolt of fabric that I later brought back to Delphine. She made me a handsome blue-and-white checked shirt with the material, which I wore for several years.

The best prizes were a pair of burlap mittens and a rabbit pelt. I had my sewing kit with me, so I turned the mittens inside-out and sewed the fur into them. Boy, were they warm! One day, we were finally issued some warmer winter boots. Decked out with my new boots, bunny-lined mittens and with empty mail bags covering my legs as I drove, I was able to survive the relatively short but severe winter. Sad to say, the bitter cold and snow posed an even more deadly risk to the infantry fighting in Belgium. The worst winter in twenty years gripped that region, killing the poorly-clad Allied soldiers at a rate nearly equal to fatalities imposed by German weapons.

One day, we were informed that the French Armored Division had punched a hole in the German line holding Strasbourg, which sits on the Rhine River bordering Germany. Reaching the river was an important strategic and psychological victory, as it left no doubt that the Allies were knocking loudly on Hitler's door. Desiring to be one of the first Americans to arrive at the Rhine, I begged my sergeant to let me join two other messengers assigned to take messages to the French Division now occupying Strasbourg. At first he agreed but then, with no explanation, he denied my request muttering something about my being "on call." I was disappointed, but my angst turned to anguish when I later learned that those two messengers never came back.

They had been captured and sent to a Nazi POW camp. Many POWs never returned from the Stalags. Earlier in the war, the Germans, who had signed the Geneva Convention, provided relatively humane treatment for Allied prisoners (compared to their savage handling of Soviet troops). However, in the last months of the war as Germany was collapsing, the POWs were not only poorly fed, clothed and sheltered, but were forced to endure brutal treatment by their captors. The maltreatment went so far as the mass murder of American GIs, most notably in the Belgian city of Malmédy, where 86 Americans were slaughtered in a frozen field on December 17, 1944. Although the U.S. soldiers had surrendered and disarmed, they were herded into a field and shot by a German assault unit. The few who refused to die right away were bludgeoned to death with the butt of a German rifle.

That incident, and three similar ones documented

that same day, happened on the second day of the Ardenne Offensive. Better known as the "Battle of the Bulge," this infamous clash took place about 100 miles north of my position. This was Hitler's last and greatest offensive effort, when he surprised us and succeeded in breaking through our thin, seventy mile American front line in the Ardenne Forest where Belgium, Luxembourg, and Germany meet. He attacked five divisions of the U.S. First Army with eight of his elite panzer (tank) units and thirteen infantry divisions. At the same time, Hitler's Waffen SS troops were ordered to fight with the utmost brutality and to show no mercy, especially toward any POWs, hence the mass murders.

Despite early victories by his line of soldiers bulging toward the American front, Hitler badly underestimated our resolve. After a month of fighting, Germany had paid a steep price for her last failed attempt at triumph: 30,000 dead, 40,000 wounded, and 40,000 captured. We suffered tremendous losses as well (20,000 dead in the biggest land battle the Army ever fought), but we were victorious, having driven the Nazis back to Germany. We had also left them sorely depleted in men and supplies, and poorly prepared for the continuing storm with the Soviets along the Eastern Front. It was the beginning of the end for Hitler.

The day after my fellow messengers had disappeared, a buck sergeant named Gaspard and I were told to head out to retrace their path toward Strasbourg and complete a message run—not a trip I relished considering the close call I'd had. It was a moonless night in the mountains, but even in the darkness the pavement suddenly looked unusually dark as we drove along. We slammed on the brakes, narrowly avoiding a

German tank trap. This huge ditch spanning the road ran 30 feet across and 10 feet deep. We very carefully and slowly turned around, knowing that most likely there were mines on either side and even more embedded in the road itself.

After having cautiously driven back some distance, we found a road off to the right and decided to try it. Though thankful to be on the right track toward Strasbourg, we were a bit jittery as we approached the city, since mines may have been planted anywhere along the way. Then we heard shelling—the Germans, positioned on the east side of the Rhine, were targeting Strasbourg. Debris from the remains of demolished buildings lay everywhere making the road nearly impassable. With nothing but rubble all around, we were clueless as to the whereabouts of the message center once we entered the city limits. Searching for someone to help us, we finally saw a French soldier standing at the edge of the street. We pulled up to him so that Gaspard, a French-speaking Cajun from Louisiana, could ask the soldier for information on the 2nd French Armored Division's location. Rather than answer Gaspard, the guy shoved his rifle in his face and accused us of being German spies; he thought that Gaspard's French was so perfect that we couldn't possibly be Americans! (As I said earlier, the Germans were masters at using languages to impersonate people, so we were suspect.) Old Gaspard, who didn't like this guy's attitude, whipped out his 45 automatic and began cussing at him. We showed the soldier the message envelopes we were trying to deliver with the French Division's name on them, finally convincing him we were legitimate. He directed us to the center located in the basement of a bombed-out building nearby, allowing us to complete our assignment. While all this was happening, shells continued to pound the city. We kept praying they weren't coming our way.

I was glad to leave Strasbourg and thankful to the Lord for protecting us from harm. But within a short distance, we were once again dodging shells. While attempting to leave a small town outside of Strasbourg where we'd just delivered the next set of messages to the 79th Infantry, shells began exploding right over our heads. They were way too close for comfort. Gaspard drove frantically for a minute and then pulled hard to the side of the road. We leaped out of the jeep and wedged our bodies between the vehicle and the wall of a building. As the black sky lit up like a fireworks finale in July, I felt sheer terror and nearly wet my pants!

We waited out the onslaught, quickly hopped back into the jeep and zipped out of there. Diving into the darkness, we tried to find a certain road to take us back to Fénétrange. We finally spotted it: a narrow, twelve-foot-wide alley that ran between two buildings and offered an alternate route out of the town. (After the war ended, those two captured messengers wrote to our captain explaining that they had taken the main road out of the town rather than the alley Gaspard and I knew to take, and had landed right in the path of the Germans. The messengers had fought until their bullets were exhausted, then they had surrendered and had been taken to the prison camp. I was relieved to hear they had made it out alive.)

One final scare greeted us as we drove through some woods on the way back. You never knew what you'd run into in the dark of night—or what you might leave behind. (One night it was so dark that I didn't even realize I'd left my buddy at the last stop we'd made as I motored off to the next town alone!) This night we came upon a huge German tank hiding in the shadows. We froze and held our breath trying to determine whether the beast was alive or knocked-out. We waited for what seemed like hours to see if there were any signs of life, but it just sat there quietly. We moved slowly, respectfully past the tank and then sped home. What an amazing feeling to lie down at last on my cozy bed, alive and able to face another day.

Some soldiers weren't as fortunate. I had to stop at a Grave Registration outfit one morning for some deliveries. Dead GIs were brought there to be identified and sent on, either to a graveyard in France or back home to their families. I was brought to a garage behind the main building and shown the bodies of a German and an American. All that was left of the American was a pair of legs and feet covered with blood-splattered pants and socks. I couldn't help but wonder where the other half was lying. The medics were unable to identify him. Typically, all your clothes were labeled with the last four digits of your serial number, so someone could figure out who you were. However, this soldier had different numbers on his pants and socks that didn't link him to any known casualties. Why he was wearing the wrong clothes was anyone's guess (though it was very likely that some miscellaneous items were given to him at the Quartermaster outfit that washed clothes for us). He was known only to God now.

Winter passed quickly in France, well, compared to home. In February, the sun began to do its work of warming the air and gradually melting the deep

snowdrifts. It was nearly time for us to pull out of
Fénétrange and cross the German border as the Red
Army, descending from the north, and Allied troops
pushing from the west, began to capture Germany city
by city. We claimed over forty miles of German territory
each day. During the last several months, I had spent
every free moment possible with Delphine. The thought
of her waiting patiently for me at the end of each
grueling day with open arms and a sweet kiss kept me
going no matter what I was facing. We'd grown so close
that I wondered how in the world I would be able to say
good-bye—not knowing whether I'd ever see her again.

Chapter Twelve

La promesse. As it turned out, there wasn't time to worry about how to say good-bye to Delphine. It ended up short and sweet, since the Army ordered an immediate departure from Fénétrange. Our convoy was leaving by noon of that day, March 17, 1945, so I rushed to gather my few belongings, tidy up the room, and hold my gal one last time. After thanking her family for putting me up those many months, I grabbed Delphine's hand and the two of us walked slowly, reluctantly, behind the chateau and down to the river's edge. There was so much to say to her. All I could blurt out was that I didn't know when I'd be back, but if the good Lord was willing, I would return. While I held back the tears, she let hers flow freely, unashamedly. I held her tight as she burrowed her face into my chest and sobbed. Glancing up I noticed the water in the river rushing by joyfully on its way to somewhere. For a second I imagined the two of us hopping into the little boat we'd shared so many times, and allowing that river to carry us far away from France, away from the war, away from the reality of this awful moment. All I could do was gently lift her face toward mine, brush the teardrops from her cheeks, and press my lips to hers one last time.

I grabbed my gear and ran to my jeep, joining the 92nd Battalion as it made its way to the Saar region, located near Zweibrucken, Germany. We didn't exactly get a warm welcome in Germany. Neither had the American soldier we found hanging in a tree as we came into the first town. Hitler's propaganda machine had convinced the people that a German "final victory" was near. However, the reality was that the Allies were to be the victors. We had liberated France rather quickly and were now standing on German soil. Her people were angry, fearful and vengeful—their wrath poured out on that hanging soldier and other soldiers who were ambushed as they entered the towns of citizens who had feigned surrender. We paid them back with heavy shelling and aerial bombing until their towns were nothing more than rubble. The rail yards near those cities were just one huge, tangled mess of engines, cars, tracks and buildings. Their homes and supplies destroyed, some of the German women tried to get friendly with the American soldiers and offered themselves in exchange for food.

We came upon city after city that had been leveled worse than any we'd seen in France. The sickening smell of corpses decaying beneath all the debris wafted up through the mounds of rock. We had to bulldoze right over those remains to make roads over which the masses of men, machines and supplies would pass on their way to the *true* final victory: ours.

After about two weeks in Germany, a small

miracle, of sorts, took place. I was ordered to take a message to...Fénétrange! Of course, I jumped at the chance and couldn't wipe the huge grin off my face as I flew down the roads and imagined her surprise at seeing my old kisser again so soon! After making the delivery, I headed straight for Delphine's house. It was getting dark as I rang the little bell mounted on the wooden door of the courtyard. My heart was pounding wildly as I waited for what seemed hours for someone to answer. She just had to be there. I had only that night to see her. What if she wasn't there? Maybe she was really upset at my leaving and had run away. Or maybe she'd forgotten me already and was out on the town with some other guy. Maybe she was sick or had been hurt or...to my great relief, the large door swung open and there she stood, bewildered, but with that bright smile on her face. Calling me "Kenny," her special nickname, Delphine fell into my arms and exclaimed that she thought she'd never see me again. After opening the door to let me park the jeep inside the yard, she and I held hands tightly while strolling into the house. As soon as we'd stepped into the hallway I pulled her toward me and allowed all the feelings I'd held inside for months to tumble out. Here she stood before me: hopeful, pure, alive, in stunning contrast to the fear, the filth, the death in the world around us. Overwhelmed by my feelings of love and gratitude for her, I told Delphine how much I loved her and that I wanted her to be my wife. Once again, tears trickled down her face as she said, "*Oui, mon chou,*" over and over again. This time they were tears of joy—both hers and mine.

   We had to make wedding plans quickly, since I had to leave the very next day. I took a piece of string and wrapped it around her slender finger to determine her ring size and sent it to my mom, along with enough money for her to find a nice solitaire engagement ring or "*diamant*," as the French called it. (My sisters, Priscilla and Thurley, ended up picking one out. It was a beauty and actually fit Delphine just right!) I had my mom mail some new clothes, which fit also, but the shoes Mom sent were two sizes too big, so Delphine gave them to her cousin.

Mom was thrilled to hear we were to be married. She and Delphine had begun writing each other those last few months of the war. My mom was relieved to hear news about me, and Delphine loved hearing about my family and life in America. Delphine's mom was surprised but not unhappy about our announcement the next day. True to form, her dad, Frédéric, simply mumbled something in French (or was it German?) and trudged out for his morning chores. I couldn't worry about him at that moment, however. I had to get to Army headquarters and apply for permission to marry. After completing paper after paper, I was told it would take at least a month to receive the necessary clearance. That was all right, since it would take at least that long for me to get back to Fénétrange. Delphine also filled out the required forms at the town hall, where our names were posted on a community bulletin board announcing our intentions. When all the papers were ready, Delphine carefully tucked them away in her bureau drawer until I could return to her and officially make her mine.

We had to say good-bye again, but this time I felt more hopeful somehow, knowing that she would be waiting for me, wearing my ring, and preparing for our life as one in the Lord. I re-joined the 92nd just in time to advance toward the large German cities of Frankfurt, Nuremburg, and Munich, plus all the smaller cities in between—or whatever was left of them.

We often traveled on the autobahn, Germany's super-highway, which made trips from city to city fast and easy. The autobahn had been used to great advantage by Hitler during the "blitzkrieg" (or lightning war), when Germany invaded Poland, Belgium, Luxembourg, the Netherlands, and the Soviet Union at the onset of the war. It later enabled the Germans to fight on two fronts: Europe to the west and the Soviets to the east.

The Nazis had also used the autobahn for an airport runway. They cleverly laid concrete between the opposing lanes to camouflage a landing strip. Their newest jets, Messerschmitt Me-262As, were hidden in tunnels or among nearby trees. Those jets were considered the fastest planes available, but they came too late in the war to do Hitler any good. While conquering Germany, the autobahn became an asset to *us*, enabling our supply trucks to race up and down it while transporting soldiers and supplies to the front lines. After delivering their loads, the trucks could pick up hundreds of thousands of German prisoners, who were either captured or who had surrendered, and take them to holding pens. (Our POW camps were overflowing at this point, so the only way we could contain all the prisoners was to place them in huge fields surrounded by armed guards.)

While driving on that freeway, I caught my first glimpse of the Austrian Alps. I was amazed to see mile after mile of heaven-high peaks covered in pure white snow. I felt strangely comforted to see that, although man could utterly destroy the buildings, roads, and bridges he had created on the earth, he could not destroy the beauty God had created in this universe. Those mountains, the oceans, the sky, and the heavens beyond would long outlive the evil deeds of man. Such deeds would, however, reach a level only Satan himself could conceive of at our next destination: a little town called Dachau.

Chapter Thirteen

$\mathcal{S}$atan smiles. We moved into some old German barracks in the small, quiet town of Dachau, on our way to Munich located eighteen miles south. Everyone was talking about the prison at the edge of town. A few days earlier on April 29, 1945, it had been liberated by the U.S. 7th Army. The unspeakable horrors discovered there would stun the world and sear into the minds of all who entered its black iron gates not only what we were fighting for but also what we were fighting against, as expressed by General Eisenhower himself.

The Dachau prison had been built in 1933 and was considered a model facility, holding mainly political and criminal inmates under more or less humane conditions. As World War II wore on, it became the first and worst of the many concentration camps, cramming over thirty-two thousand Jews, Slavs, Gypsies, POWs, the disabled, homosexuals, and anyone else deemed an enemy of the state, within its ten-foot-high brick walls topped with barbed wire.

Trainloads of captives continued to arrive

each day, even though the SS was having a hard time "processing" the current occupants, let alone the new arrivals. This process consisted of separating people into two groups: healthy men and women who could work, or infants, young children, pregnant women, and those who were old, sick or handicapped. The first group was taken to labor camp, where they slaved until too sick or weak to perform and then they were sent to die in gas chambers. The second group of unfortunate ones was herded directly to the chambers, where they were stripped of their clothing, jewelry, hair, and then the very air that filled their lungs. When the screaming ceased, lifeless bodies were dragged out, loaded onto carts and taken to the crematorium, to be reduced to ashes and chunks of bone. Day and night, thick smoke and ash billowed out of twelve smokestacks, dusting the soil with pale gray powder. Behind the crematoria where a narrow stream ran, plants grew grotesquely large and deep green, fed by a constant supply of the rich ash.

This system of extermination had gone pretty smoothly for the Commandant of the Dachau prison, a monster named Weiss, until the last months of the war when those train cars began to back up. Prisoners were forced to wait in them for three or more days, crushed together with no food, water or latrines. When the doors were finally opened, nothing but piles and piles of dead, stinking, limp bodies emerged. The Nazis, who had been desperately trying to burn as much evidence of their heinous acts as possible, were running out of coal to fuel the ovens, so the corpses just kept spilling out of the train cars and piling up everywhere, stiffening and rotting in the warm April sun. When the 7th Army arrived, Weiss and most of the regular German soldiers had fled the prison the day before, leaving behind a few SS men, as well as a scene beyond one's comprehension.

Those train cars are what greeted me as I dared to step into that Nazi version of hell. The sight and smell of the carnage turned me into another one of the soldiers walking through the camp in a stupor—silent, stunned, sick to the stomach. Clothes, shoes, and shorn hair lay in tall, individual mounds ready to be sent to a needy German populace: the hair to be stuffed into mattresses and pillows. A large bowl sat on a stool holding bloody dental instruments and bits of gold torn from teeth. I couldn't bring myself to enter the building where fellow GIs had seen the evidence of gruesome experiments on prisoners. I can't even bring myself to describe what they saw.

Hitler had no qualms about using young children to fuel his delusions of expanding the Third Reich (or empire). They became slave laborers in the camps, guinea pigs in the labs, soldiers in the field, or even training tools. There at Dachau, I saw an area used for shooting practice by German troops. The moving targets were human. The Nazis forced young prisoners to run as fast as they could across the field, only to be mowed down like wild game. Other young children in nearby towns were abducted, locked in the camp hospital, and drained of a portion of their blood to be used in transfusions for injured German soldiers. Many of Germany's own children died during this monstrous procedure when the demand became too great and their frail bodies were drained lifeless.

Several prisoners, hanging rigid and gray on gallows, were quickly cut down by our men and prepared for burial in mass graves at a cemetery outside

Dachau. The other prisoners who, remarkably, were still alive looked like walking skeletons. Hollow faces and bony hands reached out to us as they remained behind fences, many the victims of typhus, a contagious disease spread by lice. Eighteen thousand prisoners had met their fate during the last six months of the Dachau operation. For many of those remaining, weakened by months of deprivation, help had come too late. By May, over two thousand more would die from a combination of starvation and typhus, despite excellent medical care and nutrition provided by specially trained Army doctors and nurses.

Another enclosure held the DPs or displaced persons. These were people captured from various countries and used as slave labor in the prisons and concentration camps. They were forced to perform the nastiest work in the camps, such as unloading victims from the trains and carrying them into the crematoria, or removing the dead from the gas chambers and then examining still-warm body cavities for hidden jewelry or money. After the camp liberation, the DPs awaiting release exacted vengeance on an SS guard who was found cowering in the camp, then was thrown into their area. He didn't last long. Another time, I saw a large circle of soldiers surrounding a group of DPs who were tormenting two other guards. The GIs didn't interfere with the DPs, who took turns swearing at the guards, spitting on them, then kicking and hitting them. I walked away before their inevitable deaths, simply unable to handle any more brutality, no matter how well-deserved.

The question that kept running through my mind was why no one outside the camp revealed what was happening. The people of the town of Dachau claimed they knew nothing of the mass murder of thousands upon thousands who entered the prison gates but never left. (Later, some residents would admit they had suspected genocide, but felt powerless to do anything—keenly aware they'd end up within those prison walls themselves if they ever told a soul.) The horrified American soldiers who had the grisly task of cleaning out the camp, rounded up the townsfolk and paraded them through it to witness the atrocities with their very own eyes, so they'd never forget. They also forced farmers to use their own wagons in hauling the prisoners' emaciated corpses through town for all to see, then to a local cemetery. Residents were coerced into attending mass burials dressed in their Sunday best to show respect for the countless innocent victims tortured and slaughtered by their beloved "führer."

Hitler denied the world the pleasure of witnessing his ultimate defeat and our ultimate justice upon him, by committing suicide on April 30, 1945—one day after the American liberation of Dachau. However, God is just; He detests those who shed innocent blood (Proverbs 6:17). "They will be punished with everlasting destruction and shut out from the presence of the Lord and from the majesty of His power" (2 Thessalonians 1:9). "For God will bring every deed into judgment, including every hidden thing, whether it is good or evil" (Ecclesiastes 12:14).

Chapter Fourteen

Triumph. It was time for our final destination: Austria. The dust and smell of destruction and death hung heavy in the air as we passed through Munich and a few more German cities on the way to Salzburg. The Army took over an apartment building there, forcing disgruntled residents to move out. All their furniture was stored in one room, and our cots and equipment were moved in. One day, I was the only soldier there when a lovely Austrian lass sneaked into the building, saw me in the hallway, pulled me toward her, and planted a huge kiss right on the lips! Thinking I must be pretty irresistible, I soon surmised that she only wanted me to take her to the room holding her furniture so she could make sure it was still there!

A brewery a block away became our mess hall and offered plenty of free beer, much to the delight of the guys. While we were relatively fat and happy, the young Austrian children, who hung on our fence and stared at us with huge eyes while we ate our meals, were anything but. Several times I walked over and gave them everything in my mess kit. I'd rather listen to my stomach growl until the next meal than think about those little kids with nothing in their bellies and no assurance of another meal. The adults were desperate, too, of course. The garbage man would come by each day and carefully dig through our trash cans, scrounging around for bits of discarded meat or bread, or even old coffee grounds.

Spending time in the Austrian Alps was peaceful and refreshing, in stark contrast to the savagery etched in my mind. I drove up as high as I could go in the foothills one day and marveled at the drifts of dazzling white snow slowly melting and trickling down the slopes. Wildflowers of every color and design had drunk in the sparkling water and shoved their way through the remaining snow, splashing the hillside with brilliant color. This triumph of spring was a fitting metaphor for what happened next: the war in Europe ended.

On May 7, 1945 Germany surrendered unconditionally at Eisenhower headquarters in Reims, France. A few days prior to this, I knew something was up when I was ordered to drive a high-ranking officer to an Austrian town. The officer looked very sharp, dressed in his best uniform and carrying a shiny, black briefcase. I delivered him to an imposing building whose entrance was secured by armed German guards. German and American vehicles were parked in front, leading me to hope that important negotiations were being conducted. My hope was not in vain; the war was over. It had lasted five years and eight months, leaving tens of millions dead in its wake.

The shooting lasted for hours. Allied soldiers screamed and wept as they released their ammo into the air at midnight of the 8th in celebration of their hard-fought victory and its official declaration. The noise from all the gunfire was deafening, even though I'd chosen to stay inside my room and away from the window for fear of getting hit by an errant bullet during all the hoopla! I went to my knees to talk to the Lord, expressing thanks for His being my shelter, my strength, and my hope for the past months, and for His presence in the challenges yet to come.

The next morning, Vitale and I had to drive through our front lines on an important message run to the cavalry outfit in St. Wolfsgang, Austria. The Cavalry had just set free the King of Belgium, Leopold the third, and was in charge of protecting him. The King was held captive first in Germany and then Austria, after having surrendered to Hitler five years earlier and having refused asylum in England. As we traveled, I was amazed to see hundreds upon hundreds of German soldiers marching toward Salzburg from all over Germany, on their way to surrender to the Americans. They would lay down their weapons, be interrogated and informed of the conditions of their surrender, and be confined to POW camps until they could be repatriated. At one point, Vitale and I stopped our jeep, and he began to speak with a group of surrendering soldiers in their language, to make sure we were on the right road. It was strange to think that just one day earlier they would have been trying hard to kill us and now we were having a friendly conversation! Despite our new-found camaraderie, it was still scary to come upon them on the roads with weapons hanging on their shoulders. However, a close look at their faces revealed an enormous sense of relief that the war was finally over, so we continued without incident.

They were even more relieved that they wouldn't find themselves in Russian hands. There was no love lost between the Russians and Germans. We heard stories, which were well-documented, of how the Russians went into German hospitals and literally threw the wounded soldiers out of the windows and then urinated and defecated all around the hospital. We also heard of Russian soldiers who would stop trains crossing the Blue Danube River. The trains carried German civilians who were trying to get to the Americans for protection after the war ended. The Russians would take young girls off the train and drag them to a shack at the edge of the river where they'd violate them repeatedly for several days, and then toss them back on the train and grab more victims. The Soviets had sustained 26.5 million war-related deaths—the soldiers' acts were, in part, some measure of payback for the mind-boggling suffering their people were forced to endure at the hands of the Germans. I understood their fury and hatred, but didn't see how the brutal assault of innocents could avenge that suffering.

Later, we were ordered to transport three or four German soldiers to a POW camp. I silently empathized with one prisoner who muttered, "*Ich liebe nicht le Krieg.*" I hated the war, too. My empathy extended to one young German soldier I found plodding wearily along a quiet road. I should have arrested him, but simply let him continue his long journey toward home.

Driving through those mountains delivering messages was a taste of heaven: little villages nestled in

lush valleys with deep-blue lakes sparkling in the sun.
I wish I could see it again. We were in the vicinity of
Hitler's chalet near Berchtesgaden, which was referred to
as the "Eagle's Nest." He spent little time there, however,
having used it simply for show and having conducted
the last days of the war from his bunker in Berlin, the
"Wolf's Lair." I never approached the chalet, as did
many soldiers who were early "tourists" there, but heard
about its magnificent views of the mountains and its
fancy rooms. (I read that the reason Hitler rarely visited
there, coward that he was, had to do with his fear of
heights!)

After returning to our quarters in Salzburg one
night, we were saddened to hear of the death of a fellow
messenger, Jerry. He had taken his camera down to the
train yards that had been bombed. Engines and cars were
tossed around like a child's toys. Many of the trains in
the mountains were electric. Jerry climbed up on one of
the boxcars to get a better shot and accidentally grabbed
the wire above the car. It was still hot. My old buddy,
Sgt. Gaspard, was called in to identify him. He said that
the area around his heart was burnt to a crisp, while the
rest of his skin was charred and shriveled. The war was
over. This soldier never lived to tell about it.

Several other men from the 92nd and I sat
around that night, talking about Jerry, about this crazy
war and about what it all meant. The guys tended
to listen to me and often asked me to step into their
arguments or debates to be the voice of reason. Seeing
me as a Christian, who by God's grace, was not only
faithful in reading my Bible and praying but in honoring
God by the way I lived, their trust was earned. I was

able to talk freely about God being the only one who gives meaning and purpose to this life on earth and who promises eternal life in heaven through His son, Jesus Christ.

Sitting at an old piano, I began to pick out the melodies of cherished hymns learned in childhood. I remembered, as a young boy, paging through our tattered hymnals and singing song after song until my voice was hoarse! Now, way across the ocean, I began to play "The Old Rugged Cross," followed by "Trusting Jesus," and "Great Is Thy Faithfulness." While plunking out the last tune, "Softly and Tenderly," I looked up to see one of my buddies, a schoolteacher from Tennessee, with tears in his eyes join me in singing:

Softly and tenderly Jesus is calling,
Calling for you and for me;
See, on the portals He's waiting and watching
Watching for you and for me.
O, for the wonderful love He has promised
Promised for you and for me
Though we have sinned, He has mercy and pardon
Pardon for you and for me.

By the time we got to the chorus, there wasn't a dry eye in the house:

Come home, come home
Ye who are weary come home
Earnestly, tenderly
Jesus is calling
Calling, O sinner
Come home.

Thoughts of our earthly homes came to mind and, being very weary, we were more than ready to return to them and our families. I just prayed that we all were ready for that heavenly home, too, by having accepted Jesus as Savior.

"...If you confess with your mouth, Jesus is Lord, and believe in your heart that God raised Him from the dead, you will be saved. For it is with your heart that you believe and are justified, and it is with your mouth that you confess and are saved"
(Romans 10:9,10).

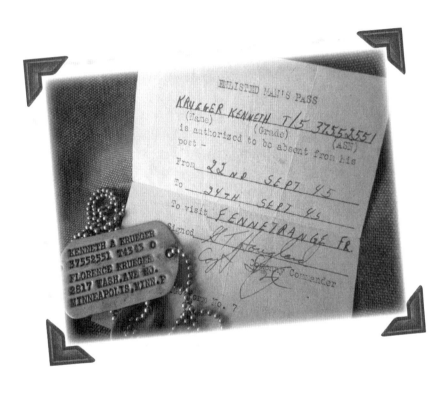

Chapter Fifteen

Pass to Fénétrange. The war was over, but we couldn't go right home as there was still much work to do over the summer. By the time September rolled around, it hit me hard that it had been months since I'd been back to Fénétrange, and I sure was missing that pretty French girl who had stolen my heart. I requested a pass from my superiors and was very surprised and glad when a three-day pass was granted. For the sake of time, I'd need to grab a train headed for Sarrebourg, France, then transfer to one bound for Fénétrange. I arrived in Sarrebourg late in the day, too late to catch the last train out. Knowing that the only way to get there now was by foot, I started off for the ten-mile trek. It was sweltering that afternoon and I became boiling hot and terribly thirsty while running as fast as my legs could go, but the thought of holding Delphine again kept me moving.

I finally stood at her door, exhausted and gasping for air. Once again, she was overjoyed and a bit shocked to see me. She squeezed me tight and kissed my red, sweaty face over and over, saying how much she loved me and had missed me. I wasn't feeling very good at that moment, but her wonderful welcome made me forget the searing pain in my lungs and the constant throbbing in my head—for awhile, anyway.

I woke the next morning relieved to be back in my comfortable bed upstairs, but realizing that something was terribly wrong. I could barely talk, and it was so hard to breathe that I felt suffocated. My body wasn't sweating any longer but was burning up, and my head thumped to the pace of my racing heart. And it wasn't just because Delphine was in the room! We guessed it was pneumonia. A doctor was called in but never showed up. Delphine and her mom took care of me that day and late into the night. They did everything possible to cool and hydrate my body. To clear my breathing, sips of watered-down schnapps were given. The two "nursemaids" weren't sure I'd pull through. I drifted in and out for several days, being vaguely aware of their presence, but sensing that I was in good hands: theirs and the Lord's.

My three-day pass had long expired when I turned the corner and began to feel better. I had to find a doctor who would write the Army a note explaining my two-week absence. Being deathly ill wasn't exactly how I'd imagined my time with Delphine, but I was blessed to be alive and on the mend. Another blessing was that during the last days of my recovery, we had time to finalize our wedding plans before I returned to my unit. It would be a simple ceremony at the church in town with her family and friends in Fénétrange. Her best friend, Celeste, and her brother, Etienne, would stand up for us. Her mom was already busy sewing up a pretty dress for her from some pale-blue fabric (which symbolized purity) given to her by a cousin.

Delphine had started *la trousseau*, French for "bundle," which held her best clothes, nightgowns, undergarments, and linens she would take to her new home in America. She didn't have much. The family was quite poor due to the war, but she took pride in what little she did own. Delphine had also begun to embroider our initials on some of the linens—letters K and D intertwined with a larger K for Krueger. Her dad couldn't have been too disappointed about me—at least I was German like him (well, half-German, anyway), and would give her a proper surname. He didn't say much of anything about our plans, though. I sensed he went along with things for his daughter's sake.

Delphine excitedly told me about French wedding traditions and symbols, several of which I knew were popular in America, as well. The morning of our wedding, Delphine would take a long, fragrant bath to purify her for the wedding and to wash away all thoughts of her past life and past loves. She would put on her blue dress, carry orange blossoms in her arms, and wear some blossoms in her hair. I would walk to her home and escort her to the church on foot, preceded by musicians and followed by her family. As we made our way, children would stretch long, white bands of cloth across the road ahead of us and my bride would cut each ribbon, which stood for the trials of life we would overcome together.

The scent of flowers and incense would fill the church as we were escorted to red velvet chairs. The ceremony would take place under a silk canopy, representing protection from harm. A kiss before the congregation would seal the deal, and then we would walk across a path of laurel leaves for success in marriage. Church bells would clang wildly, heralding the entrance of a new couple into the world. Well-wishers would toss seeds or bread at us, wishing us wealth and fertility, and throw coins, or *dragées* (candied almonds) to the children.

The reception would be simple, with the two of us sharing a drink from *la coupe de mariage*, usually an heirloom, two-handled cup in which a piece of toast would be dropped (the "toast" to the couple), ensuring a healthy life. We would then share the traditional dessert, *croquembouche*, a pyramid of small cream puffs drizzled with caramel glaze. That last tradition might be hard to come by, though, as things such as sugar were nearly impossible to get. I told Delphine I'd try hard to find some sugar for her but couldn't promise anything.

I didn't look forward to the final tradition—*la chivari*. This was when a group of friends appeared at the door or under the window of the couple on their wedding night, and banged pots and pans until the couple came out and invited them in for snacks and drinks, celebrating until late into the night or early morning. After everything we'd been through, I knew I'd just want to have Delphine all to myself that special night!

Delphine was anxious to set the exact date we'd marry, but I kept warning her that I couldn't be sure when I could get another pass to come back for the ceremony. She said it would all work out and insisted on confirming a date, which we did. We would be married one month from that day, on a Saturday morning. I made it very clear, though, that things could change and that the wedding date depended entirely on my getting a pass. She nodded that she understood and gave me a great kiss, which would have to sustain me for a whole month!

I made my way back to Salzburg and reported in, counting down the days until we would become husband and wife. I applied for the precious pass and tried to keep busy to make the time go by faster. As the big day approached, I realized that I hadn't received that pass yet and went to check on it. My head started to spin as I was told, matter-of-factly, that the request had been denied. Not believing my ears, and trying hard not to panic, I went to the next officer-in-charge to see what the hold up was. I pleaded with that guy, trying to help him understand that I was going to get married in a week, but he coldly dismissed me saying I could re-apply later. Anger and disappointment grew in me until I had visions of choking that creep! What was I going to do? It was too late to get a message to Delphine about the delay. I felt awful, but took comfort in the knowledge that I'd warned her about possibilities like this, and had to trust that she would take it in stride and postpone the festivities until the day I could get there.

That day finally arrived, two weeks later, when the pass was suddenly given to me. I quickly gathered my things, including a ten-pound bag of sugar for Delphine that I'd wrangled from our sympathetic mess sergeant. My Army buddies were nearly as relieved and happy as I was. They patted me heartily on the back and wished us well. I sprinted to the train for France, which would take me back to Strasbourg and then to Sarrebourg, where I'd catch another train for Fénétrange. Of course, it seemed to take forever to get there. The noisy, rickety old car crawled across the Rhine and slowly lumbered into France. Finally catching sight of the faded blue sign that announced *Fénétrange*, I leaped off the train while it was pulling into the station. There was a half-mile walk to her house, but I felt as if I were stepping on air at that point. I found myself standing before her door again, nearly shaking with anticipation. This was it! She was finally going to be mine—forever. Just as I'd imagined many long months ago, we could actually hop in that little boat on the river behind the chateau and let it carry us far away, to a new place, to a new life, to new joy.

I rang the bell and smiled at its very familiar, comforting sound. No one came after several minutes, so I rang it again and tried to wait patiently, while feeling like jumping out of my skin! I heard soft footsteps approach the door and watched it slowly open. She seemed glad to see me as I wrapped my arms around her slender waist and drew her to me. I held her tight for a few minutes and then pulled out the bag of sugar and presented it to her with a slight bow. Now we could have that special treat for the wedding reception. Instead of the brilliant smile and expression of surprise and delight I expected, Delphine quietly, calmly, firmly stated that there would be no wedding.

Chapter Sixteen

Fighting for Delphine. I felt my knees go weak at her words. I sensed the bag of sugar slip through my fingers and plop to the ground. The bag split open, spilling its precious contents at our feet. She stared at the ground, not daring to meet my eyes, knowing the disbelief and hurt they would reveal. I lifted her chin, forcing her to look at me. She said nothing, but tightened her lip. I asked her over and over what was wrong, but my questioning was met with silence and a hint of defiance. She didn't really have to say anything; I knew what was wrong.

Anger began to surge within me. Delphine had been told repeatedly that I couldn't guarantee I'd make it back for the specific date she'd insisted on. She had said that she understood and that everything would work out. Had she gone ahead and prepared for our wedding day anyway? Had the church been decorated and had the pastor written our vows? Had the food and drink for the reception been purchased? Had she bathed and dressed and waited for me with a bouquet of orange blossoms in her arms that morning a week ago? I understood how she would feel abandoned and embarrassed, but was she so mad that she would refuse to marry me now that I was standing there before her?

While these questions ran through my mind, she finally spoke, stammering, "*Mon père, mon père!*" She went on to say that it was her father who forbade her to marry me now. When I kept asking why, she refused to answer. Again, I could understand how he would think I was a jerk for not showing up, but hadn't she told him that I might not get back when she'd planned—that I was at the mercy of the Army to allow my return? If so, couldn't he understand that? No doubt the family had gone to some time and expense they could ill afford in order to give their daughter a decent wedding, but it wasn't my fault. I had given her fair warning.

I sensed something else behind the refusal, though. Was my failure to show simply a convenient excuse to get rid of me? I knew that her father hadn't liked me from the moment I came down those stairs and first laid eyes on Delphine. Now he had a valid reason for detesting me. But there must be more to it. I begged her again to tell me why her father said no. She continued to stare at the ground. After what seemed an eternity, she finally murmured, "*La lampe de poche.*" Flashlight. Flashlight? What in the world did that have to do with anything? She let out a deep, heavy sigh and explained that the first time her father met me, his eyes instantly honed in on the many notches dug along the bottom edge of my flashlight handle. It took a minute to dawn on me; some guys would cut notches into their tools to mark off the weeks or months or, quite possibly, the number of rivals they had killed. Did her father assume that I had made such a death tally on my mine?

Again, he may have had uneasy loyalties and, though no fan of Hitler, was empathetic toward his own people. He probably thought I had dispatched quite a few of them and was eager to brag about it. Little did he know that I had never even shot my gun throughout the entire war (except for practice) let alone killed any Germans! How could I make her father understand the truth? He'd never believe me.

At least I knew that calling off the wedding wasn't all Delphine's idea, and was hopeful she still loved me. I tried to calm down long enough to figure out what we could do. It was hard to think straight, but I came to realize that we possessed the necessary papers, and simply needed someone to make it legal. I told her we could go to her minister or even the Army chaplain and be married that very day. She refused to give the idea a thought, insisting that she wouldn't go against her father's wishes. I pleaded with her to pack her things and slip away with me, but Delphine was adamant that she could not and would not disobey her father. She half-heartedly said that maybe we could get married some other time. Some other time? What was she thinking? I had a whole week's pass in my hand, and the honeymoon was to take place in a nearby town; all she had to say was, "I do." All she *could* say was maybe some other time? It was hard to believe this was happening. With the war in Europe over and my job winding down, it was a matter of days before I'd be shipped home. I'd planned to proudly take my wife with me. Now what?

Most of that week is a blur in my mind. I hazily remember riding bikes along the narrow roads and through the deep woods to her relative's house, only to sit there feeling empty and numb. We spent the evenings with her parents, just as we had that past winter. I tried hard to pretend nothing was wrong, while seething inside with anger and resentment toward her father. I should have been on my honeymoon with my beautiful bride, and here I was playing card games in the kitchen with her grumpy father! Finally, I just lost it. Bolting from my chair and flinging my cards at the table, I began screaming at Frédéric that it wasn't fair: here he'd had two wives and was denying me even one! He just sat there in his stubborn, stoic manner, staring straight ahead. He ignored my tirade and refused to tell me why he stopped our marriage. I stomped off to my room, enraged at him, and not too proud of my own behavior.

My pass was up the next day, and I'd have to leave. Feeling so hurt and depressed that I wasn't sure I even wanted to see Delphine that night, I went to bed early. (Secretly, I hoped she would come to me, but she never did.) After a fitful sleep of an hour or two, I got up and headed down the hall toward the bathroom. Suddenly, someone was coming toward me. It was Delphine. She stopped abruptly, startled to see me. The hallway was unlit except for the moonlight pouring though a side window. The light made her shoulders, still moist from a bath, shimmer in the darkness. Her lovely shape was only slightly veiled by a thin towel she held around her, revealing feminine curves I'd only seen in a dream. I walked toward her and gently gathered her to me. She shivered a second and then seemed to melt into the warmth of my body. I held her close, thinking that it would have been like this on our honeymoon— that it could have been like this. I kissed her lightly on her soft neck and once again breathed in the lingering fragrance of lavender. It was all I could do (especially considering that I was a red-blooded American boy who was *supposed* to be on his wedding night) to release her and let Delphine head toward her own room, alone, as I dejectedly made my way down the hall.

I left early the next morning, before anyone was awake. Upon arriving back in Salzburg, my buddies were all excited to hear about my marriage and eager to congratulate me. It was so painful to admit that we hadn't married at all, and that my fiancée's father was the one who'd ruined our plans. I don't know what the men thought—they just felt sorry for me. And as I'd suspected, a few days later we were instructed to turn in our guns and head home. We joined the 3rd Battalion of the 313th Infantry Regiment, along with guys from various outfits, to begin our journey out of Europe. I should have been thrilled, but I knew that I'd also be on my way out of Delphine's life, possibly forever.

I began to panic and tried to figure out what one could do to buy some time. The only possibility was re-enlisting. If I had more time in France, maybe then I could somehow convince her dad I was worthy of her. But where do you go to sign up again? I hurriedly went to Company Headquarters, then Battalion Headquarters, and finally Corps Headquarters, but no one knew how to go about it. They must have thought I was nuts for wanting to stay behind. Frustrated beyond words, I returned, crestfallen, to my unit.

Before we left Austria, we were given a final task: that of capturing Nazis who were hiding in private houses in the area. We approached one town's mayor, who quickly revealed the soldiers' whereabouts. Rounding them up one by one, we escorted them to prison, surprisingly without much resistance. I think they knew they'd be well-treated by the Americans, receiving adequate food, shelter and medical care, despite the fact that the Germans had starved, tortured and even killed our POWs.

It was autumn when we finished that job and were ordered to leave the Continent. We loaded into trucks and headed for the train yard in Salzburg. Hundreds of soldiers there clamored into box cars, creating a line stretching four blocks long. Everyone on board was grinning from ear-to-ear as the train pulled out—everyone but me. My face registered sorrow, deep sorrow, that I had won the war but had lost the battle, as they say. I was going home—without my Delphine.

Chapter Seventeen

Dire adieu. As the train made its way back through Austria and Germany, all I could do was think of her. I methodically ate and slept, hopping out of the train for a brief comfort stop in the woods on occasion. We soon crossed the old Rhine River, once again via that rickety bridge. I looked way down into the water rushing below and prayed we wouldn't end up in it! The bridge had been bombed and rebuilt just well enough to get trains across. The train creaked and swayed as we slowly passed over, and then steamed toward Strasbourg.

Now that we were in France, it was just a matter of time until we'd arrive in Sarrebourg, just miles from Fénétrange. I closed my eyes and prayed silently to the Lord. I began by praising Him for His amazing love and gift of salvation. I then thanked Him for having brought me through this war alive and in one piece. Finally, I asked Him for wisdom in deciding what to do next. As my eyes opened, the train was slowing and pulling over for an express train to pass. The soldiers were able to quickly visit the woods or pick up food and souvenirs at the station in Sarrebourg. I jumped off along with the other guys—only I never got back on. Instead, I ran to the depot to check on the next train to Fénétrange. The box car I'd been in began to pull out as I bought my ticket to my "home away from home." My fellow GIs wouldn't notice old Kenny missing until they were well underway and heading toward the Army camp in Marseille, France.

My heart pounded while I was boarding the train—in an hour I would once again be holding her. I would also be considered AWOL by the Army, but all that mattered was seeing Delphine one last time and saying a proper good-bye. After arriving in Fénétrange and running as fast as possible, I soon found myself at her door. She opened it within seconds of my ringing the little bell. You should have seen the look of surprise on her face! In an instant, she was wrapped in my arms once again.

We walked arm-in-arm into the house and entered the cozy kitchen, where her parents were sipping the last of their morning tea. You should have seen their jaws drop! After greeting them and before her father had a coronary (or punched me out), I quickly assured him that I was on my way back to America, but had decided to risk getting in trouble with the military in order to say farewell to Delphine. I wanted desperately to talk with him, to reason with him, to even beg him to allow us to be married. But it was too late now. My military status was already in jeopardy, and I would risk further discipline by the Army if I went AWOL any longer. I also feared that if I said anything, Frédéric would get angry and kick me out, stealing the precious moments

I had left with his daughter. We had a single day to be together, as I would need to leave very early the next morning to try and find a fast train going to Marseille; and with any luck, catch up with my troop train.

That evening, Delphine and I sat on an old, wool blanket next to the river and shared a simple meal of bread, cheese and pears. We talked and laughed and kissed as the sun slid beyond the horizon, washing the sky with gold and giving Delphine's face a warm glow. I tried to memorize her: her long, wavy hair fluttering in the breeze, her shiny smile and full, pink lips, those sparkling, delphinium-blue eyes that pierced right through my heart. Her strong yet delicate hand slipped into mine as we watched the sky dim to dark blue, then to black. As we gathered our things and headed toward the house, we noticed another glow on the horizon and ended up watching the moon rise, bright white and majestic. It slowly took its position in the sky and cast a moon glade toward us, which glistened across the water and landed at our feet. We kissed one last time and said good night.

Morning arrived, just as cold and gray and dreary as I felt. I said a final *au revoir* to Delphine's mom and dad, and then she walked with me toward the train station. It began to drizzle about half-way there, so I asked her to stop and turn back toward home, since the depot was still several blocks away. We held onto each other for dear life. I couldn't help it—I started to cry and told her I was afraid I'd never see her again. Delphine pulled away from me for a second and a terrified look came over her face. She knelt down and clung to me exclaiming that I just had to come back someday. She begged me to promise that I would return. She wouldn't let me go until I did promise. I gently pulled her up, looked deep into those sad eyes and gave her my word that one day I would come back. We shared one last kiss and then I began to walk away. It was a sorry, sorry day to leave her there outside of Fénétrange. I remember glancing back as she stood in the road, looking so forlorn and miserable. Her slight frame was dwarfed by an oversized raincoat, but still I could see her shoulders quake as she sobbed. Her tears mingled with the heavy raindrops now falling and streamed down her face.

It took every last bit of strength I had not to look back again. I had to focus on meeting up with the box car I'd abandoned. Relieved to catch a fast train to Marseille, located on *la Côte d'Azur* in southern France, I began to search for my troop train. As the train stopped at towns and cities along the way, I anxiously peered out the windows in hope of coming across it. Even though I had been gone a day, the chances of my catching up to the slow-moving locomotive were in my favor. Sure enough, later that afternoon, the troop train was spotted on a side track. I vaulted out and ran down the platform until I found my box car. Immediately upon boarding, who should greet me, but the captain of our car! I could have lied and said that I'd been left behind at another station, which was very possible, but he was owed the truth. I told him what I had done and why. He was very understanding and, rather than turning me in, issued his own sentence: I would be in charge of making sure all the latrines at the Army camp in Marseille were squeaky-clean! (It wasn't a very severe punishment. My hands never even touched a scrub brush since the cans were actually cleaned each day by German POWs.) We remained at the camp for more than a week and, since there wasn't much to do there, I was given permission to see the sights in Marseille. Walking along *La Canabière* (nicknamed "Can o' Beer" by the GIs), a wide boulevard leading to the Old Port area, a huge sign caught my attention: RE-ENLIST HERE—GET A 30 DAY FURLOUGH! I couldn't believe my eyes. Here I had been asking everyone possible where to go about it, and the opportunity was right in front of me! Now what? I didn't know what to do. As much as I wanted to be with Delphine again, if I were to re-enlist there was no guarantee I'd continue to be stationed in Europe. The war was still raging with Japan, and I could very well be sent there, as had many others. Even if I were to be stationed once again in France, what if her father continued to deny me Delphine's hand in marriage? I'd be stuck in the Army again for nothing! I also yearned to go home. It had been two long years since I'd seen my family and was missing them and my country more than words can say.

Pausing, I thought long and hard about what to do. I took a deep breath and walked past the recruitment office. It was time to go home. Perhaps I could go back for Delphine once I was officially discharged from the Army and had resumed civilian life. Besides, what did I have to offer her now? With no job, money or even a high school diploma, her father would never relent. I tried convincing myself that getting a job and saving money so I could return to her was the best plan. Still, it was impossible to shake the sadness of having to leave her for now.

The time came to ship out. Our vessel was loaded with men and supplies and then began to cross the Mediterranean. She streamed past the Rock of

Gibraltar, and then surged onto the Atlantic for the long voyage home. It seemed strange to be on a single ship surrounded by nothing but deep-blue ocean and light-blue sky. I felt even lonelier, considering that when we had come to Europe over two years before, we were part of a huge convoy of thirty-six ships that kept us company. My fellow soldiers on board now were unusually quiet—lost in their thoughts, memories and hopes. My own melancholy mood shattered as the sky suddenly turned charcoal and gusty winds whipped a hefty spray of icy saltwater across my face. The waves swelled and sloshed across the deck, shoving me off balance while nearly washing me overboard. I grasped the security rope, pulled myself over to the nearest exit and flung my body to safety below-deck. It would have been sadly ironic if having survived the sickness, the vehicle accidents, the craters and tank traps in the roads, the scorching days and freezing nights, the Tiger tanks, the Stuka dive-bombers and their 500-pound bombs, the artillery shells, the land mines, the snipers, the Nazi soldiers, and yes, the bad food, I were to end up bobbing in the middle of the ocean as shark bait!

We experienced rough seas the entire week of our journey, but surprisingly few of us became sick this time. I guess we'd all toughened up since our first trek across. Toward the end of the seemingly endless trip, I kept scanning the horizon for any glimpse of land: our land. Finally, I could make out a dark sliver lying at the edge of the sparkling stretch of water. We all began to yell and clap so loudly that I bet our joy and relief echoed across the miles and could be heard all along the coast! As our beloved America loomed larger and larger during our approach, I couldn't help but think about the men and women who were not returning with us. It was because of their ultimate sacrifice that we could see our country and its people still alive, still beautiful, still free. Those of us on the ship would be honored as heroes, but even greater heroes were left behind. Their blood had bought liberation for millions of precious souls and freedom for decades to come. America would remain the land of the free *because* of the brave, as a slogan which is popular today reminds us. I also thought about the parallel with Christ's sacrifice on the cross. His blood was shed to liberate us from the tyranny of sin and Satan—and to offer *eternal* freedom for all who believe.

After our ship docked, we went briefly to one camp, then were sent to Camp McCoy in Wisconsin. With official discharge papers in my hand dated December 13, 1945, as well as a Bronze Star, a Meritorious Medal for heroic duty (message delivery while under fire), and some other decorations, I finally boarded a train to Minneapolis.

After the train pulled into the old Northern Depot, I put on my heavy overcoat, threw my big duffel bag over my shoulder, walked to the nearby streetcar track and waited for a car bound for my house on 29th and Washington Avenue North. Although it was just past five in the evening, it was nearly dark out and quite cold. People walking by glanced at me and smiled or even saluted. When the streetcar came, I climbed the steps, dropped my fare in the box, walked to the back of the car and leaned against the rail. Peering out the windows I watched all the familiar streets, houses, shops, cafés, parks and churches fly past. It was comforting to see that nothing much had changed while I was away. What had changed was me. The war had forced me to grow up fast. Long gone was that innocent kid who had proudly worn a crisp, new uniform, shown it off to his family, and left his home to save the world. In his place was a man wearing that same uniform, which was now faded and worn. A man who returned home wise beyond his years, keenly aware of both the depravity of man and the deliverance of God.

I recognized my street and pulled the cord for the next stop. Just as on that night when I'd left over two years earlier, the streets were dark and nearly deserted. Once again, the arc lights overhead cast their pale yellow light and guided my steps toward home. I made my way up the still-crumbling sidewalk, grateful that several lights were glowing through the windows, and opened the porch door. The front door itself was locked, so after knocking and while waiting impatiently for someone to come, I began to notice the warm, wonderful aroma of mom's cooking filling the chilly air. It was so exciting to be back that I'd forgotten my hunger and heard my stomach roar. Then the door swung open, and my mom stood there astonished. (No one knew I was even back in the States!) She exclaimed, "Oh, Kenny!" and then threw her arms around me and gave me a huge hug and kiss. I'll never forget that moment: safe at home at last. The next words out of her mouth were, "Are you married?" The look on my face gave her an answer she did not want to hear.

After nearly inhaling mom's food I'd been dreaming of for years, we talked late into the night. The whole family was there, except my sister, Priscilla, who had married and moved away. They had many questions about my experiences in the war, but all I wanted to talk about was that pretty French girl I adored. My mom adored her, too, and was very disappointed that we hadn't tied the knot yet. However, she accepted my assurance that we would be married as soon as we could work it all out. While falling asleep that night, warm and secure in my old bed, my only thought was of Delphine and those things I'd tried hard to memorize: her soft hair, her sweet lips, her lavender-blue eyes and her warm, slender hand in mine.

Chapter Eighteen

Jamais plus. I never saw her again. I sit
here recalling and writing down those bittersweet
memories, some sixty years later, and ask myself why.
Why didn't I return to France? What happened to her?
Did she marry and have a family? Was she still alive
after all these years? These questions began to torment
me as I entered my ninth decade of life, after having
read a memoir written by a fellow soldier from the 92nd
Battalion. In that book, the soldier painfully shares
the story of his engagement to another young woman
from Fénétrange. They, too, were planning to marry.
He completed his final assignment in Austria, and then
happily raced back to Fénétrange, only to learn that
his fiancée was dead. She had been savagely raped and
murdered by three Nazis.

I felt profound sadness for his loss. I hadn't
thought about my beautiful French girl for many years,
but that moving account brought a torrent of memories
and questions about Delphine. I found myself crying
off and on for weeks for both his loss and mine. Then

determination set in to find her. First, I had to search my memory, letting myself go back to the time right after we had said that final good-bye...

Upon returning from war, I took a part-time job as a busboy at the Oak Grill, a fancy restaurant at Dayton's Department Store in downtown Minneapolis. It was great working there, since I was given meals as well as a salary. The thick, delicious malts provided helped me gain back some of the weight lost while living on Army rations. Working very hard that first year, I saved as much as possible for our wedding and our future.

During the summer of 1946, I took some time off to teach children enrolled in Bible school at several rural churches across southern Minnesota. It was great to see the smiles on those bright faces as they listened intently to God's Word and sang His praises. The kids reminded me of the children in Europe, whose faces would light up with the simple gift of a chocolate bar, an orange or a hug. I wondered how they were faring in the aftermath of the war and prayed that their basic needs for shelter, security, food and medical care, which one can easily take for granted here, were being met. I also prayed that someone there was telling those precious souls the truth of the Gospel: that Jesus loved them so much that He was willing to die for their sins, so they could have an eternal relationship with God on earth and in heaven.

Realizing my love for teaching people about God, I looked into going to Bible college to train as a missionary. Although I had left school early for the Army, Northwestern College, located in Minneapolis at the time, allowed me to take an entrance exam and accepted me as a student. (Evangelist Billy Graham would later become president of the college from 1948-

52.) The GI Bill helped to pay for my full load there, but I also quit Dayton's to work full-time with my dad making bolts at Lewis Bolt and Nut Company. As the hot summer winds began to cool and coax the leaves off the trees, my freshman year began. I attended class every morning, then worked the three-to-midnight shift. Studying was squeezed in there somehow! I always made time to write to Delphine and couldn't wait to arrive home in the wee hours of the morning to tear open her letters and digest every word before flopping down, exhausted. My mom continued to exchange letters with Delphine as well, expressing her hope that the two of us would be re-united soon. She loved her nearly as much as I did!

I had been home almost a year before realizing that the intense memories of death and destruction witnessed during the war were dimming a bit. In their place were fresh memories of warm, joyful times with friends and family. One day, a special joy, unbidden and unexpected, would become life-long. My brother, Gordy, had met a beautiful young woman named Mae. He was interested in dating her and thought of inviting her to a movie show, but he learned that she didn't attend shows. I rarely did, either, so he figured we would be better companions. Gordy decided to introduce her to me, and the rest, as they say, is history. To this day, I don't know how it happened. From the moment we met, Mae and I saw each other every single day, except one, up until our wedding day on September 12, 1947. My brother was amazed and teased that I never even gave her time to take a bath!

Again, I don't quite know how it happened. I certainly hadn't intended to date, let alone fall in love with anyone else. Maybe I was a bit lonely. Maybe I was still deeply disappointed and hurt that Delphine had gone along with her father—feelings of anger and bitterness toward him gnawed away at me. Or maybe I sensed that, as much as I loved Delphine, it wasn't in God's sovereign plan for us to marry. Or maybe it was simply that right before me was another lovely, smart, funny, sweet, Christian girl with whom I could share my life. Maybe all those things.

As my relationship with Mae began to grow, my letters to Delphine slowed and then stopped altogether. Her letters kept coming, but in time I sensed she knew something was wrong. She tried to sound cheerful, but her words hinted at a quiet desperation. I knew I had to write one last letter telling her the truth: that I had met someone else and that I was not coming back. My mother was livid when she heard I'd broken up with Delphine. As I said, my mom adored her and now her dream of our marriage was destroyed. I could imagine how Delphine would respond. She had been writing and waiting for me for over a year, only to lose all hope in a letter that began, "Dear Delphine, I'm so sorry...." Surprisingly, she was very gracious and understanding. In writing back, she wished us all the best and politely asked whether she should return the gifts and the ring I'd given her. I told her that I wanted her to keep everything. My mom and Delphine continued to correspond until 1956, when my dear mother died and went home to the Lord. During their writing back and forth, Delphine would still ask my mom about me once in awhile, and my mom would tell me a bit about Delphine, but I never heard from her again.

After Mae and I married, we rented a small apartment in Minneapolis, one block from Loring Park. I worked two jobs back-to-back, from seven in the morning to midnight. We soon had two children. For awhile I returned to Bible school and quit one job. We moved to a larger rental home in Circle Pines, but I was still gone all the time, and poor Mae was overwhelmed being alone all day and evening with two small kids. I chose to withdraw from college and spend more time with my growing family. We bought our first house, a three-bedroom rambler for $11,150 on a GI loan. We were blessed with five wonderful children: Terry, who is now in heaven; Tom; Cheryl; Jim; and Paul, with whom I now live. I also have ten grandchildren and fifteen great-grandchildren who bring so much love and joy into this old soldier's heart. My dear Mae and I served each other and the Lord for fifty-five years until her death from heart disease on her birthday, January 12, 2002 at the age of 75. I must have cried every day for a year after she went to Glory.

Several years later, after reading that fellow soldier's memoir in 2005, it was time to mourn that very first love of my life, Delphine. I felt I just had to find out what had happened to her, but where to begin? I went to the local library to do some research. After finding the addresses of both the American and French Ambassadors, I wrote letters to them requesting help, but received none. Next, I spoke with a very empathetic French woman at the French Consulate in Chicago. Although touched by my story, she couldn't help due to the limited information I had about Delphine. She gave me a few numbers to call in France, but again they were dead-ends. I shared the story with my son, Tom, in Alaska and with my brother, Russell. They each searched the Internet for organizations that help people find others, but those services cost way too much for me. Finally, my brother, Russell, had an idea and helped me write a letter of inquiry to the postmaster in Fénétrange. In it, I explained who I was searching for, including the names of all her relatives I could remember from sixty years ago. With the help of his computer, Russell translated the letter into French and sent it across the Atlantic with the touch of a key.

This seemed my last hope. I prayed that the postmaster would recognize one of the names I'd sent and be able to supply an address or forward my letter to that party. I tried to wait patiently for a reply and thought about what else could be done, short of an actual trip to France, to find her. One thing I did do was get my passport, just in case I would have a chance to go see her again. But was she even alive? If so, what if she was married? I decided I wouldn't contact her in that case and just be happy in assuming she was doing well. What if she was a widow? Would she want to see me after all these years? I would love to look into those eyes again, their brilliance softened with time, but still full of life. If she'd agree to meet me, what if we fell for each other again and had that wedding after all? (My wife used to say that I'd probably remarry before she was even cold!)

As I daydreamed, Russell received an e-mail. The postmaster in Fénétrange had found the address of Delphine's brother, Etienne, living in nearby Sarrebourg, and had forwarded my letter to him. I couldn't believe we finally had a lead! I hoped he'd have some recollection of me back in 1945 and information about Delphine. It was agonizing to wait for over a month for a response, but I was elated when a letter from France arrived. Curiously, the return address showed that it wasn't from Etienne, but from a woman named Elise. My heart nearly burst through my chest with anticipation as I opened the letter. Then my heart just broke. It had been written by Delphine's grandniece and began, "Dear Ken, I'm so sorry...my great-aunt, Delphine, is dead." She passed away from cancer at the age of 73 in 1999. Once again, I was too late. After pausing to wipe my eyes with a trembling hand, I began to read the rest.

Elise went on to say she was absolutely shocked to have heard from me after all those years. She said that I was sort of a legend in the family: the handsome American soldier who was to have married Delphine after the war. The story of our courtship and engagement had been passed down through the generations and was seen as so romantic; to me, it was so tragic. Nearly as devastating as learning of her passing was what Elise shared next. She said that Delphine had never forgotten her love for "Kenny," and went on to explain what had happened to her great-aunt after receiving my letter breaking our engagement. Several months before that, Delphine had realized that I most likely would not return for her, and the last letter I sent helped her accept that— at first. When it really sank in, she became inconsolable. Her family tried everything they could to help her, but it wasn't enough. Desperate, they sent her to an aunt in Nancy, France, and then to another one in Switzerland, to see if they could comfort and encourage their niece. It was no use. Still shaken and sad, she left Switzerland and simply wandered the next few years, eventually ending up in Paris working as an *au pair*, or nanny, for a family there. Six years later, in 1951, she met and married her husband, Georges, who lives in Sarrebourg to this day. Elise said that they had had a wonderful marriage and were blessed with three daughters, ten grandchildren, and many great-grandchildren. I was very thankful to know that.

I was also deeply saddened to know she was gone. I envisioned her ever-lovely image encased in a cream-colored stone frame on top of her grave in a small churchyard, much like her mother's. Those amazing eyes would still be as blue as the bouquet of delphiniums arranged lovingly beside her picture. Within the grave would rest her still form and upon her lap, one delicate hand would be gently placed across the other— a hand never to be taken in mine in marriage. I felt as if I'd lost a second wife.

A sense of guilt began to eat away at me for having abandoned her. Not only had I broken my promise to return, I felt convicted that I had failed God, as well, by disobeying His will that I marry Delphine. I thought back to the time when we were together in Fénétrange. We believed in our hearts that we were married and simply needed the official license and ceremony to confirm it all. Had I broken not only my promise to return but also holy vows, understood yet unspoken?

I wrote to Elise explaining my side of the story and expressing regret at what I'd done. I also shared the story with my other kids and older grandkids. They had no regrets about my not marrying Delphine, having realized that they wouldn't be here were it not for my marriage to their wonderful mother and grandmother, Mae! However, they did understand my grief and guilt about how I'd treated Delphine.

The only way to end the torment was to repent of my behavior long ago and of all the anger and resentment I'd harbored these many years toward Delphine and her father. It was, sadly, too late to ask their forgiveness, but as a believer I knew one could always approach God. First John 1:9 states: "If we confess our sins, He is faithful and just and will forgive us our sins and purify us from all unrighteousness." After many months of agony, I tearfully bowed before the Lord and humbly confessed. Immediately sensing His presence and pardon, I knew that my sin was now removed as far as the east is from the west, as promised in God's Word. And though still grieving her loss, I now had peace with God and the peace *of* God would, in time, ease my heart until the day I joined my loved ones in heaven.

Another Bible promise I claim is: "...that in all things God works for the good of those who love him, who have been called according to his purpose" (Romans 8:28). I don't always understand this truth, but I have seen evidence of it throughout my life; today I am blessed in having a special long-distance friendship with Delphine's brother, Etienne, his wife, Nathalie, their granddaughter, Elise, and her family, who all live in France. We exchange letters, pictures, birthday and holiday cards, as well as gifts. It has been my privilege to have prayed for their family members, including Delphine's children, grandchildren, and great-grandchildren throughout the years, and I am so glad to know that many have trusted Jesus as their Savior. As long as there is breath in me, I will continue to pray that *all* will place their faith in Christ and praise God for His gift of eternal life. As for this life, I guess that you never quite forget your first love.

Epilogue

Ken Krueger shares a home in Blaine, Minnesota, north of the Twin Cities, with his son, Paul. At age 83, Ken remains faithful to his desire to serve the Lord by involving himself in several ministries at his church. He works on a Missions Committee and is a member of the Council of Servant Leaders. His continuing commitment to children is evident as he shares weekly Bible stories with young children at a daycare center located in the church, and teaches kids in Vacation Bible School during the summer. Ken is known and appreciated as a "Prayer Warrior," who earnestly intercedes for individuals in his family, community, and around the world.

Ken loves spending time with his children and extended family and enjoys many hobbies, such as gardening, fishing and boating, studying war history, and cooking. He is a wonderful chef, often showing up on a friend's doorstep with his delicious turkey chow mein, baked salmon, pumpkin bars, or apple crisp in hand!

One of Ken's dreams is to return to Europe and drive once again across those roads he knew so well even in the dark of night. While in France, perhaps he could at last satisfy his promise to Delphine and offer a final good-bye to the special girl who offered love, comfort and hope to a young soldier so far from home.

Return to Fénétrange

"The bitterest tears shed over graves are for words left unsaid and deeds left undone."* World War II veteran, Ken Krueger, can attest to the truth of this quote—he has known such tears. Yet at the same time, he has tasted some of the sweetest ones possible. Tears that surge from deep inside, primed by profound relief that, at long last, those words *were* uttered and those deeds *were* done. I will never forget witnessing that moment when tears of remorse merged with those of redemption after years of regret. It is my honor to share that experience and more as I continue telling Ken's story in the second edition of *Fighting For Delphine*.

The reader will quickly note that "Delphine's" true name is revealed: Marguerite. Ken lovingly refers to her as Margie. I was unable to secure permission to use her real name, or the names of family members, in time for publication of the first book. However, her family has since granted approval. For clarification, the pseudonyms used in the first book are indicated initially in parentheses.

In *Return to Fénétrange,* another change will be evident—the additional chapters are written primarily from the author's perspective, enhanced by direct quotes from Ken and others we met along our journey. They shared bittersweet memories of Ken and Marguerite's love story, as well as vivid accounts of war-torn France. These recollections and insights are essential to the accuracy and poignancy of both parts of the book. My long-held desire was to take Ken back to France, where time seemed to stand still—not only to fulfill Ken's dream of returning, but to see with my own eyes the people and places I had only seen through his. It is by God's grace that both my desire and his dream were realized. "Delight yourself in the LORD and he will give you the desires of your heart" (Psalm 37:4).

I am forever grateful to my husband, Greg, who took exceptional care of Ken, transporting him in a wheelchair across France. Filmmaker Troy LaFaye was invaluable in capturing moments of an adventure that astounded us all. A special "thank you" is extended to our families, friends, and contributors who have supported this effort. We greatly appreciate our new friends we met while in France—they graciously opened their hearts and homes to us, and made a Minnesota soldier feel proud of his service to secure life and liberty for generations.

May people here and abroad read about and remember Ken as one who represents the everyday yet extraordinary soldiers of the "Greatest Generation." May we never forget the sacrifices that were made in the name of freedom—sacrifices made for *our* freedom.

*Harriett Beecher Stowe

Chapter One

Le Retour

"God's gifts put man's best dreams to shame."* Ken Krueger had just one dream at this time in his life: to see France again. At the age of eighty-six, with little money, little relief from chronic pain, and little ability to walk more than a few feet, the old soldier held little hope of ever returning. God had a gift for Ken—against all reason, against all wisdom, against all odds; he was on his way there.

Ken slowly, carefully packed new slacks and shirts into his suitcase. The task was made difficult by the blurring of his vision as he thought of her. Had it really been nearly seven *decades* since he last held Marguerite (Delphine)? Last kissed her? Last breathed in her scent of lavender? Last heard her pleas for him to return while fiercely clinging to him in the cold, relentless rain?

As he gently placed a well-worn brown leather Bible on top of the clothes, the very same book that provided hope and comfort to him throughout the war, one question begged for an answer. Yes, he was elated at the thought of retracing his paths as an American Army motor messenger, but honestly, *why* was he going back? As much as he would delight in driving along the roads he knew so well and in seeing once more the country that was his home for nearly two years, the truth was, Marguerite was gone.

No longer could he prove to her that he had fulfilled the promise to come back and make her his bride. No longer could Ken ask her for the forgiveness he so desperately desired. Returning now made very little sense. Yet one thing compelled him to do just that: his sense of honor. Throughout his life, Ken strove to live honorably. After having sought God's wisdom and guidance, he was successful in nearly every way—except in the way that would matter most to a young French woman clinging to her first love.

At the very least, a trip back to France would allow him to say that he had indeed kept his promise to return, albeit too late to be of any real consequence. He could perhaps restore his broken honor but never her broken heart. For this, guilt and shame continued to vex him. He knew beyond a doubt that he had repented, and that God had forgiven him for his failure, giving him peace with his Savior. Did he dare believe that God was allowing this opportunity, so that in going back he would once and for all forgive himself and *experience* that peace?

Ken finished packing by tucking in carefully chosen gifts for Marguerite's family members, who were anxiously awaiting his arrival in France. He had been writing to them for six years, after having found her brother, Charles (Etienne), and his wife, Marthe (Nathalie), alive and residing in Sarrebourg, France. The town was about ten miles from Fénétrange and not far from where Marguerite was buried.

Both men were anticipating a joyful reunion—Charles and Ken had not seen each other since they were teenagers in the war. Charles represented the closest link to his beloved Marguerite. Ken hoped that his old friend would be able to shed more light on his sister's life after the war.

Ken had also corresponded with Charles' and Marthe's granddaughter, Lisa (Elise), who helped translate the letters they had exchanged over the years. She was fascinated by the romantic story of her great-aunt, having been told the sad tale many times throughout her childhood. Lisa shared, in her own letters to Ken, some of what happened to Marguerite after Ken left on that bitter day in 1945—knowledge that both warmed and chilled Ken's heart. He longed to hear more firsthand from Lisa and to meet her family, whom he had known only in photos: Lisa's husband, Tim, and young children, Vianne and Jean.

The French family was delighted that this great American "legend" was actually coming to meet them. Yet one concern loomed in all of their minds: should they tell Marguerite's husband, Gérard? He still lived in the couple's apartment near Strasbourg, France, and frequently kept in touch with the family. Charles and Marthe had decided not to tell him about Ken's letters during the last six years, not knowing whether Marguerite had ever mentioned anything about Ken to her husband. Although Ken and Marguerite's engagement had ended well before she met Gérard, sudden news of his wife's old flame showing up in Fénétrange might prove to be greatly disturbing to any man—especially to one quietly, resolutely living out his last years in a flat saturated with memories of his beloved wife. It was nearly inevitable that Gérard would hear about this special visitor. Out of respect and kindness, he needed to be told the truth.

Ken slowly pulled on his new army green canvas jacket, and then flipped on his hat—the "magic" hat as it would later be called. Ken had gone to a military supply store before the trip to find something for his head. He chose a baseball cap, which had the words "World War II Veteran" proudly blazoned across the front. Little did he know that the hat would play a vital role in opening doors for him, time and time again, as he traveled ahead to the past. He lugged the heavy suitcase across the living room floor to wait for his ride to the airport. Just as in the Army sixty-seven years ago, Ken would need to "hurry up and wait" often during the next couple of weeks as he made his way across the Atlantic and back.

Ken was heading to France with me, the author of his memoir; my husband, Greg; and filmmaker Troy LaFaye. I would gather information and still photos for the second edition of the memoir, Troy would shoot a high-definition video documenting Ken's return, and Greg would enable Ken to travel safely from Minneapolis, Minnesota, to Reykjavík, Iceland; from Reykjavík to Paris, France; Paris to Fénétrange, France; Fénétrange to the Normandy Coast; and then back to Paris to begin the flight home.

How was this finally happening? After *Fighting For Delphine* was published in 2008, Ken and I, often accompanied by Ken's son, Paul, traveled around Minnesota sharing his story at numerous World War II events and book signings. Ken was honored to meet hundreds of fellow veterans and their families at various venues. An instant camaraderie and rapport was apparent as the soldiers locked eyes and shared memories, both the amusing and the agonizing. Other folks graciously extended a hearty handshake, voiced words of gratitude for his service, asked for a hug, or even gave a kiss on the cheek. One deep, persistent desire of Ken's, which he expressed often as he shared his stories, was that of returning to France.

I longed to make that a reality for him, but it seemed impossible. Or was it? Considering Ken's age and health, if a trip were to ever happen, prudence suggested it be soon. After much thought, prayer, and a leap of faith, I decided to take Ken back. Appeals were given, fundraisers were held, and Ken made personal appearances at military events and on local television and radio. Articles on Ken's story also appeared in newspapers and magazines, all in an effort to raise money for the trip overseas. Despite widespread publicity, donations simply trickled in. Nevertheless, Ken refused to give up hope that he would step on French soil once again. He had confidence that if it were a part of God's sovereign plan for him, it would come to pass. And it did! A travel itinerary was created, contacts were made in France with the family and the media, and a loan was secured to supplement the gifts of others who shared our vision of helping Ken return to France.

Actually getting there would prove to be more challenging than imagined. Ken, Greg, Troy, and I arrived at the airport in plenty of time for our evening flight, only to learn that it had suddenly been delayed. The airport at our stop-over destination, Reykjavík, was closed due to volcanic ash being spewed into the air by the Grimsvoten volcano, which had begun erupting the day before. Ironically, our plane was called "Eyjafjallajokull," named after the largest volcano in Iceland. It had blown its top in 2010, plunging the country in total darkness, imprisoning people in their homes, closing roads, and stranding millions of passengers across Europe as flights were cancelled. After a lifetime of waiting, after years of prayer, after endless hours of planning and preparing, we feared meeting similar circumstances.

To everyone's great relief, the flight was cleared to leave after two anxious hours of waiting. The airport in Reykjavík was still not open, but was scheduled to do so an hour before our landing, *if* visibility improved. We had settled into our seats feeling somewhat more hopeful, when it was announced that the departure was delayed yet again—this time due to mechanical failure. Though the rest of the passengers began to buzz about their suspicion that this flight was not meant to be, Ken sat quietly with his eyes closed and spoke with his Heavenly Father. His prayer ended with a verse from scripture, one among many, which Ken had long ago memorized: "This is the confidence we have in approaching God: that if we ask anything according to his will, he hears us. And if we know he hears us—whatever we ask—we know that we have what we asked of him" (I John 5:14).

Not long after the final "amen" was uttered, we heard the announcement that the plane would depart for its six-hour trip to Keflavík International Airport in Iceland. Ken was filled with gratitude. Now he could ease into his window seat and wait for sleep to overcome his thoughts. The lateness of the hour and the soothing hum of the engines should have lulled him into deep slumber, but anticipation of what lay ahead precluded any real rest. He did not mind, though, because a few hours later he became a witness to night slipping seamlessly into day. While the rest of the passengers dozed, Ken watched in awe as the moon shimmered across the plane's wing. Then mere moments later, the sun began to inch its way up through the horizon, ever so slowly illuminating Ken's face with a burnt orange glow. He marveled at this colorful display of God's majesty.

Ken began to sense the plane's descent at the same time another wonder appeared in the window—a vast, alien landscape of bare, volcanic rock topped with an occasional craggy hill. Stony deserts, sandy wastelands, and steaming hot springs stretched as far as one could see. Lonely, single-lane roads slithered across the basalt rubble leading, seemingly, nowhere. The sun quickly fled as a shroud of thin, gray smoke engulfed the plane. Tall, wispy plumes of deeper gray smoke rose from single mountains in the distance and formed menacing clouds of ash that hung heavy in the air. It was not until the plane approached the runway that there appeared to be any life in this barren land, curiously called Iceland. Low-growing shrubs shared the roadside with purple Nootka Lupines and were the only evidence this was still earth. Intrigued by the scene, Ken was oblivious to a minor miracle—that we were indeed landing. The atmosphere had cleared just enough to allow the airport to re-open in perfect time for our arrival, despite the protestations of an angry volcano.

The passengers were quickly herded to the next plane bound for Charles de Gaulle Airport in Paris. After another five hours of sleepless expectation and a long, painful walk down the jetway, Ken, somewhat in disbelief, stepped onto French soil once again. By this time he was exhausted, hot, dehydrated, out-of-breath, and aching. But he was there. His dream had become reality after sixty-seven long years of waiting and wondering, of praying and pleading—what a gift from the Lord. However, throughout this trip, God would bestow several more gifts upon Ken, which would prove to be much greater than any mere dream of man.

*Elizabeth Barrett Browning

Chapter Two

Bonjour Paris, Encore Une Fois !

After landing, going through customs, and being escorted through the airport, our team stuffed a wheelchair, luggage, and film equipment into the largest rental van available. We drove another hour to a bed and breakfast in the quiet town of Linas, France, just south of Paris. The quaint, stone *chambre d'hôte* located on a narrow, cobblestone street would serve as our base for the next several days.

Moved by our apparent weariness, the gracious hosts offered to prepare a simple dinner for us. We were famished and eagerly accepted. While resting on a cool, flower-filled patio and waiting for the meal to be served, we marveled that we were finally in France. This fact became abundantly clear when the "simple meal" prepared for us turned out to be a gastronomic delight, as is the reputation of French cuisine. A salad of delicate leaf lettuce from the host's garden, drizzled with tangy Dijon dressing, was served first. This was followed by a crunchy wedge of endive with the same delicious topping.

Next came slices of warm quiche, rich with cream and Gruyère cheese. The main dish was the most tender roast beef imaginable, having simmered all day in wine and herbs. The meat was enhanced by a currant sauce, and was served with a side of spaghetti and crusty homemade bread.

After everyone was ready to explode, the host re-appeared, bearing bowls of incredibly rich ice cream smothered by a warm ganache that defies description. Needless to say, sated and sleepy, we four collapsed into our beds and did not move until morning. We had to be awakened the next day so as not to miss yet more amazing food served during *le petit déjeuner*. Breakfast consisted of croissants, yogurt with granola, fruit cups, crêpes with ham and cheese, and fresh strawberry or raspberry juice. Ah, "*Vive la France!*"

The itinerary the first day involved taking Ken to see la Tour Eiffel. He had not laid eyes on it since that day in August of 1944, when throngs of euphoric French women had bestowed hugs and kisses upon a handsome American soldier. Driving into Paris was quite a nerve-wracking experience as vehicles charged down the freeway mere inches from each other. Out of nowhere, motorcycles roared behind us, paused ever-so-slightly, and then flew around the car on both sides, zipping along the impossibly slim space between the lanes. One cringed, imagining the carnage if one of the vehicles ahead were to decide, suddenly, to change lanes. The concrete walls aligning the motorway assaulted our eyes with dizzying displays of neon graffiti. After exiting the freeway, our proximity to fellow drivers remained the same, but the pace slowed somewhat as the tree-lined boulevard flanking the

River Seine ushered us to the foot of the Eiffel Tower.

Thankful for a close parking spot reserved for the disabled, Ken was wheeled to the square beneath the massive structure. Thousands of visitors were stacked shoulder-to-shoulder. It reminded him of the day he had stood there among an ecstatic crowd, three days after Paris had been liberated. At that momentous time, the American soldier had felt privileged to not only be witnessing history, but to be playing a small role in it as well. What a thrill to stand there once again.

Our team was daunted by the blocks-long line of visitors waiting to get a ticket to the tower. We were pondering the wait, when a French military officer approached us. After noticing Ken's Army jacket and hat, he grabbed my arm and took me to the front of the line, literally shoving aside weary patrons, so that I could purchase tickets. Next, he escorted our group past an equally long queue of sightseers waiting to get inside, through a private door, and onto the elevator crammed with people who had waited several hours for this experience. To our amazement, within minutes we found ourselves standing on the second level of the tower looking at Paris below in all her glory. Ken knew this was one of God's gifts to him.

Never having been *in* the Eiffel, Ken remarked that he had never seen Paris like this! He recalled how he had driven her streets, had seen her churches and monuments, and had gazed at her rivers and fountains during his brief swing through Paris. To see it all spread out before him now like a vast, magnificent kingdom was *tout simplement merveilleux*. A biting May wind blew into his face as he slowly circled the platform while pointing a shaky finger toward iconic sites. Montmarte, le Sacré Coeur, l'Arc de Triomphe, l'Hôtel des Invalides, le Cathédrale de Notre-Dame, and la Rive Seine sat in dissonance to modern skyscrapers and high rises soaring in the distance. Despite the fact that they were 380 feet or nearly 30 stories above the street, the sounds of cars, motorcycles, buses, and the clip-clop of horse-drawn carriages reverberated upward, lending a sense of reality to the surreal scene below.

Just as when he had seen the Eiffel for the first time, Ken felt thankful he could enjoy the tower. You will recall how the military governor of Paris had been ordered to destroy it, along with the rest of Paris, in keeping with the Fuehrer's scorched-earth policy. Hitler would rather leave a city of burning bodies and buildings behind than to let it fall intact into the hands of the Allies. At the risk of his own life and that of his wife and children, the governor defied the direct order and lied that he had already begun blowing up the newly-liberated city and her people. Although the governor was responsible for the misery and deaths of countless people throughout the war, many French citizens still considered him to be *le sauveur de Paris,* or savior of the city.

The following day, the team decided to walk along the rolling hills and winding paths of the famous cemetery, Père Lachaise, on their way to l'Arc de Triomphe. The eerily beautiful cemetery, named after King Louis XIV's confessor, was inaugurated in 1804 and spreads across 109 acres of the northeastern corner of Paris. A massive stone wall protects more than 70,000 elaborate mausoleums and tombs, along with the columbarium (holding cremated remains). Thousands of trees, flowering plants, and bushes as well as spectacular brass, stone, or marble works of art surround the tombs. Exploring the grounds is akin to experiencing a lovely old outdoor art museum. However, one should not forget that each tomb honors someone's beloved parent, spouse, child, friend, or hero.

Several of the more than one million people buried there are revered icons of art, science, theater, literature, music, and history. Chopin, Rossini, Molière, Hugo, Wilde, Colette, Piaf, Bernhardt, plus American rock star, Jim Morrison, whose grave is one of the most visited, are among the well-known residents of *la cité des morts* (city of the dead), as it is affectionately called by the French. Our team was fascinated by the vast personal and public history represented there, as are the two million people from around the world who visit the cemetery each year.

After lunch at a Thai restaurant, where Ken was treated as a special guest and addressed as *le général* by the owner, we drove up the mile-long Champs Élysées. The famous broad boulevard, with perfectly-groomed horse-chestnut trees, begins at la Place de la Concorde to the east, and leads to la Place Charles de Gaulle and l'Arc de Triomphe to the west. Once touted as "*la plus belle avenue du monde,*" with its luxury specialty shops, cinemas, and quaint cafés, the street now more resembles an American shopping mall, complete with McDonald's. Some French citizens lament that it has lost its soul. Ken simply wished he could magically bring all the people back from 1944. They had once jammed the road, giddy with relief after being released from four interminable years of oppression during the German occupation. He would have loved to see their radiant faces again, and to witness the outpouring of unbridled joy made possible by Ken and his fellow liberators.

On that day, however, he saw only a busy thoroughfare jammed with motorcycles parked at its flanks, and a parade of vehicles flowing toward the Arch. Well-dressed couples walked leisurely arm-in-arm; professionals in impeccable business garb scurried up and down the sidewalks; and tourists in jeans and tennis shoes meandered between the shops and restaurants. Ken was determined to join them. He asked to be helped out of the wheelchair and began the long, painful walk to the Arch with the aid of a cane in each hand. As he inched his way up the walk, a few passers-by noticed his veteran's cap and gave him a thumbs up, while another called out a "thank you." Others, curious about the video camera following him, paused and observed Ken's persistent pilgrimage toward the country's monument to victory, surmising they had happened upon a special moment in time for this American.

After walking several blocks, something he had not done in years, Ken came to a steep staircase leading under the street and to the Arch. Crossing the street via the underground pedestrian tunnel was the only way one could safely get to it. Undaunted, Ken began to slowly make his way down step by excruciating step, while gripping his canes and wincing in pain as his arthritic knees threatened to buckle. While intensely concentrating on negotiating each of the dozens of steps, Ken began to be stopped briefly by people ascending the stairs.

Seeing his "magic" hat, they greeted him or gave him a pat on the shoulder. He smiled back despite the gnawing sensation in his legs, and continued to descend.

As soon as Ken finally reached the bottom, an enthusiastic young man approached the old soldier, who by then was struggling for breath. The student had observed Ken's hat and, in a heavy French accent, explained that he had a relative who had fought during the Normandy invasion. The young man was a World War II reenactor, who portrayed a Canadian army soldier and was excited to meet his first American veteran. He had a flurry of questions for Ken and asked to have their photo taken together. This was the first of many encounters with people across France who recognized that Ken was a returning war veteran and honored him as such.

We began walking along the tunnel and came to a group of eight French soldiers dressed in camouflage suits with yellow-fringed epaulets. They stood at attention with guns at their sides. Ken walked right up to them and attempted to speak using the vestiges of French he had learned during the war. He tried his best to explain that he had been a Motor Messenger in the 92nd Signal Battalion, and that he had fallen in love with a beautiful French girl decades ago. They did not appear to comprehend, but did recognize that he was an American soldier and agreed to have a group photo taken. Sitting on a long bench were several elderly French soldiers dressed in deep blue military jackets festooned with colorful medals. Once again, Ken tried to converse but was met with a barrage of incomprehensible French words. He simply smiled and nodded back.

Ken was so engrossed in the attempt to communicate that he had ignored an urgent need to "See Mrs. Jones," as he calls it. Ken asked the men where he could find the nearest *toilette*. One obliging man with a moustache seemed to understand and motioned him to follow. Our foursome blindly followed him up yet another arduous set of stairs, and upon reaching the landing, was astonished at the sight. This was no restroom. An immense plaza under the Arch lay before us, buzzing with activity. Dozens of blue, red, and white French flags rippled in the wind. Hundreds of military officers sporting blue or red berets and jackets adorned with multi-colored ribbons and shiny medals strode across the plaza. French dignitaries dressed in perfectly-tailored jackets with white cravats, dark glasses, and fedoras stoically observed the frenzied crowd. More soldiers with navy hats trimmed in red stood at attention, with their rifles and bayonets at their sides.

Several French citizens proudly displayed their own flags—one tiny boy helped his father by holding onto the bottom of their tall flag pole with all his might. Another hundred young people chatted and laughed together at one side of the square. Heaps of bright flowers were strategically placed at one end of an area where people seemed to be assembling. A band could be heard practicing marching music in the distance.

Before we could even attempt to explain our true destination, we were taken through the rope barrier and quickly ushered to a staging area. There, we were urged to join a long line of people. Quite bewildered, it slowly dawned on us that we had been mistaken for participants in some sort of ceremony. Later, we found out that we had indeed stumbled upon a celebration at the Tomb of the Unknown. Originally, the tomb symbolized those who had died during World War I, but now honors those who died in WWII and all subsequent conflicts.

While sitting in the chilly air and still desperately needing to visit "Mrs. Jones," Ken struck up a conversation with a young French couple. Upon hearing Ken's story, they sincerely thanked him for his role in liberating France and were fascinated by his sad love story. Ken realized he was standing in line with the families of fallen French soldiers, as well as alongside French veterans. They were chosen as special guests to witness the laying of a memorial wreath at the Tomb of the Unknown and the lighting of the eternal flame, as is done in America. The couple was there to see the young man's grandfather honored for his service in WWII. Ken was there, by God's design, in the midst of it all.

Ken felt the crowd engulfing him as the festivities began. Realizing this, two petite, elderly French women standing behind him took it upon themselves to guard Ken. They each firmly grabbed a handle of his wheelchair and glared at anyone daring to step too close. Ken managed to peer through the fray and saw that before him was the very tomb: lying flat, outlined with copper bricks, and inscribed with the words, "Ici repose un soldat Français mort pour la Patrie 1914-1918."(Here lies a French soldier who died for his country...) An eternal flame of yellow and orange, which is re-kindled every evening at 6:30, flickered silently in the breeze as twilight approached.

The crowd hushed as the band began to play in earnest.

The musicians marched into the plaza and took their places along its edge. A soldier carrying the French flag approached the tomb, along with a police officer who saluted the grave. Several young people bowed and then presented two enormous bouquets of flowers, one orange and one yellow. From the other end of the plaza a processional began—twelve heavily decorated soldiers proudly carried their beloved flags to the tomb. Next, several dozen teenagers took turns solemnly bowing, and then placing massive bunches of purple irises at its base.

The former Army Chief of Staff, le général Bruno Cuche, stepped forward brandishing a sword. He and two of the students touched the sword to the flame and then to the grave. Next, the general and several officers lined up and offered salutes to the flags and the tomb. Ken joined the salute with tears cascading down his cheeks, thinking of all the brave men and women here and in his own country that had never made it back home. The band began to play "*La Marseillaise*," the French national anthem, and the crowd began to sing, "*Allons enfants de la Patrie/Le jour de gloire est arrivé!*"

After the final notes echoed across the square, the dignitaries began to shake the hands of invited guests in the receiving line. The procession was led by General Cuche. Ken saw him coming his way. It would indeed be an unexpected honor if he could meet a five-star French general. Ken was afraid the high official would miss him as he sat in the chair, so he struggled to stand. He thrust out his hand in anticipation of a handshake, although he was aware that each person was receiving a simple nod from the general. He stopped in front of

Ken, looked him directly in the eye and, in perfect English, politely stated that while he was appreciative, he did not need to stand. Ken explained, "I had to shake your hand. I wanted to stand to salute you." The general paused while looking thoughtfully at the expectant hand. He then removed his white glove and accepted Ken's firm grasp. No doubt curious as to why the gentleman with an American Army hat was in attendance, he noted with surprise in his voice, "You're an American."

"Yes, Normandy," was all Ken could muster in this brief exchange. Cameras began to flash wildly as the two greeted each other. One photograph would later be published in several French newspapers. In fact, several articles with photographs would be published in different papers across France highlighting Ken's trip, much to the humble Ken's amusement and delight. The general produced a warm smile, donned his glove, and then moved on.

After a dozen other dignitaries shook Ken's hand and proceeded to greet a line of young French servicemen, the band broke the relative silence with a recessional tune and the crowd began to disperse. Instantly, Ken was surrounded by people with broad smiles offering handshakes and asking to have their picture taken with him. He was surprised and even pleased by the attention, yet did not want to distract them from the real focus of the ceremony: the young, unnamed soldier lying in a tomb just a few feet away.

As soon as everyone began making their way back into the "City of Light," Ken wheeled himself to the foot of the tomb, bowed his head, and quietly prayed. The soldier, representing many thousands more lying in shallow, unmarked graves, may have been unknown to France. However, there are no soldiers unknown to God. The young man was well-known by his omniscient Creator, who loved him and gave Himself for him. "God demonstrates his own love for us in this: While we were still sinners, Christ died for us" (Romans 5:8).

With twilight losing its strength, Ken was determined to see more of the Arch itself before dark. He began rolling himself beneath its grand walls which soared 162 feet above his head and stretched 150 feet across and 72 feet deep. This monument, completed in 1836 to highlight France's military victories and to honor those who fought for France, especially during the Revolution and the Napoleonic Wars, is magnificently adorned with artwork. Six bas-reliefs are sculpted on the façades and depict significant moments in war history. Above them is an intricate frieze of a battle scene— musicians are drumming and trumpeting the soldiers on horseback into battle, while brave generals lead the way. Inside the arches are engraved the names of major French battles, victories, and generals. Four elaborate sculptures, grand in stature, protrude from the base of the columns.

Ken sat alone awhile and craned his neck upward to view these incredibly beautiful representations: the French rallying against foreign invaders; Napoleon as conqueror; a soldier defending his family; and a celebration of peace. Ken was not only in awe of the monument, but also of the fact that he had been unwittingly included in the French ceremony.

God's sovereign plan and timing are perfect. It had been quite a day, but He had one more gift awaiting Ken.

Our team assembled at the top of the staircase leading back to the tunnel and under the insanely busy road circling the Arch. Ken dreaded the very thought of the agonizing walk down endless stairs with his knees and bladder already burning, but there was no other way to get back to the car. Ken was startled when a female *gendarme* appeared from nowhere and tapped him on the shoulder. Seeing the uniform, he wondered whether he had done something wrong. "Would you like to cross the street?" she inquired. We looked at her quizzically, thinking we had misunderstood. "Would you like to cross the street?" she asked again. "*Mais, oui!*" was our reply, but still her meaning as to exactly *how* she intended us to do so was unclear. She could not possibly mean that we should attempt to walk across the largest roundabout in the world where twelve avenues branch out from the traffic circle. There were no crosswalks, no stoplights, no discernible lane markings, no "yield to pedestrians" signs. It would be akin to crossing the Indy 500 track with hundreds of race cars charging toward you. Simply observing the mad dash around the Arch was both amusing and terrifying.

The officer motioned for us to follow her and yes, that is precisely what she was suggesting. She called another officer over, blew her whistle, extended her hand toward the first car she confronted, and then stepped off the sidewalk. Magically, the car stopped just inches from her. Thinking she was either the craziest or bravest traffic officer ever, perhaps both, we had no choice but to trust her. We timidly ventured onto the pavement. She blew again, held up her hand toward the next vehicle approaching, and it screeched to a halt as well. She continued to order the vehicles to stop one by one as she traversed the street and they obeyed—an impressive feat considering the speed at which they were traveling. Greg pushed Ken in the wheelchair, I walked apprehensively behind them, Troy scrambled to catch the moment on tape, and the second police officer held the cars behind us at bay. Ken thought the whole thing was spectacular and began cheerfully waving to the drivers as if he were the Grand Marshal of a fine parade. Unamused, no one waved back.

After parting the Red Sea of traffic and safely delivering her followers to the other shore, the gendarme blew her whistle again while motioning the vehicles forward, permitting the traffic to swarm once again. Ken was so tickled she had stopped traffic for him, on arguably the craziest intersection in Europe, that he thanked her profusely and offered to give her a kiss. She diplomatically replied that a hug would do and accepted a quick embrace before calmly resuming her duties.

We simply stood on the other side for a minute, a bit stunned, and then burst into laughter—we could not believe what had just happened. Our jovial mood suddenly sobered, though, when it mutually dawned on the three of us that Ken never had found "Mrs. Jones," and that it had been *hours* since he was desperate to meet her! Knowing time was of the essence, we spied the McDonald's further down the Champs Élysées, grabbed Ken's chair and sped toward it. He held on for dear life as we weaved in and out among startled pedestrians. Ken finally, gratefully made her acquaintance there, much to everyone's relief.

Chapter Three

Souviens-Toi

It was time to say *à tout à l'heure* to Paris. The next morning our team began the 280-mile drive east to Sarrebourg, France, in the Alsace-Lorraine region. Ken would finally see Charles, who was then a retired primary school headmaster. Time, distance, and Providence had separated the two men for a lifetime. In one day's time, God willing, they would be reunited.

Ken could not help but wonder whether Charles would even recognize him after so many years. No longer was Ken the epitome of a young soldier—tall, strong, agile, and quick. His legs were now bowed due to arthritis having eaten away the lining of his knees. His hands, calloused and wrinkled from years of hard work, shook as he clutched his wooden canes in an effort to steady his hunched frame. His face bore creases etched by the heartaches and joys of a life that was full and well-lived.

Time and trials could not diminish those lively, lovely blue eyes, however. Their color and clarity appeared to intensify as Ken took in the French countryside flowing past the car window. An emerald fabric of rolling hills, with tiny villages nestled in its folds; quaint farms with stone silos atop its ridges; and azure lakes deftly placed in between, elicited praise for its Creator. At one point, our foursome stopped to visit one of the numerous herds of cows enjoying the lush grass of a pasture. We had discovered the secret of those incredibly rich dairy products enjoyed in Paris—happy, friendly cows! Unlike American cows who slowly back away when one approaches and look at you with disdain, the French *vaches* came right up to us, jostling each other for a good look. They seemed to smile and say, "*Bienvenue!*" or welcome. No wonder there is a brand of French processed cheese products named "*La vache qui rit*" (the laughing cow).

They were *not* terribly friendly to each other. Another day, our team had come across a curious sight—a dozen cows playing "King of the Hill." One cow stood defiantly on the top of a tall mound of dirt. Its rivals would circle around, and then groan and stomp up the hill in an attempt to displace the "King" and claim superiority. It was comical to watch their game as the king (more likely, queen) stood her ground by unceremoniously pushing her foes back down the mound with her head and broad shoulders. The losers were persistent, nonetheless. Having regained their composure after the humiliating slide back down, they would trudge up once again, undeterred. If successful, a loud bellow announced the triumph, just like a boastful professional wrestling champ claiming victory.

Back on the road, Ken began to sing a medley of songs he had learned during the war, which transported him back to another era. He recalled most of the words, but on occasion his voice would trail off as the lyrics left him. He would pause briefly and then launch into a different ditty. One tune in particular seemed to touch Ken, reminding him of all the young men who had never made it back home: "My Buddy." "Nights are long since you went away/How I think about you all through the day/My buddy, my buddy/Your buddy misses you."

The first stop would be Lunéville, where the gut-wrenching German attack on unsuspecting civilians had occurred. You will recall how children on their way to school, and many other townsfolk just beginning their morning, were brutally blown apart by German 88mm shells while crossing the bridge leading into town. Today a modern, new bridge spans the narrow river. Looking beyond it, one can see the remains of the bridge decimated by the enemy—half of it still extends from the land, crumbling slowly into the waiting water. The other half is conspicuously absent, as are the hapless victims. Gazing at the blue water flowing peacefully beneath one's feet, it is horrifying to envision the same river tinged red with the blood of innocents.

We continued on to the next town of Tarquimpol and to a bed and breakfast located in the Regional Natural Reserve of Lorraine. The B&B, le Château d'Alteville, would serve as a base for a few days for three of us. Gracing the grounds are two mansions from the 16th and 18th centuries; le Lindre, the largest trout pond in France; a 500-year-old organic farm; and not to mention several resident storks.

The Château has a rich history, including having been occupied by the German Army during the war. After Germany had taken over Poland, Denmark, Norway, and Holland, it turned its sights on Great Britain and France. The Battle of

France officially began on May 10, 1940, with the German blitzkrieg blasting through Luxembourg and Belgium. The French knew they were next. Having assumed an attack would take place along its eastern border with Germany, the Maginot Line was set up as a defense. The Line was a series of forts backed up by pillboxes (concrete bunkers surrounded by barbed wire) and connected by underground tunnels. French troops were concentrated there as well. The Germans outfoxed them, though. They attacked France at the northern end of the Line, having gone through Belgium and the Ardennes—a heavily-forested area of hills believed to be impenetrable and where French troops were sparse. Paris was taken weeks later on June 14, 1940.

D'Alteville's owner and gracious host, David Barthélemy, related that in 1939, prior to the Battle of France, the Germans had begun infiltrating the Lorraine area. His widowed grandmother, who resided in the Château, was forced to flee the property. She left with nothing but her seven children, ranging in age from three to thirteen. The family took a train to southwest France where a house requisitioned by the state awaited them. They remained there safely until the end of the war.

In addition to housing enemy soldiers, the Château was used as an agriculture school. Its new functions most likely saved it from destruction, a common fate of many historic homes. Several architectural changes were made to the residence to make it more functional and in tune with German aesthetic tastes. All of the classic French hip roofs, known for their steep pitch, were completely removed and rebuilt in a simple, flat German style. New corridors were installed, the fireplaces were replaced by faience heaters (ceramic stoves creating radiant heat), and the wood floors were covered by colorful ceramic tile.

Despite this "desecration," the heirs to the estate are grateful that the basic structure was preserved and restored. The lovely home is still enjoyed and appreciated today by their family members and many guests. Lying in a four-poster bed and looking up at the high ceilings and fabric-covered walls of one of the five charming guestrooms, it was chilling to imagine it having been occupied by a German soldier long ago.

Most of the mansion's original furniture, paintings, and books, which were already quite valuable at the time, were saved by a shrewd uncle. He used a false certificate he had forged to enter the property. Boldly, he removed the items and took them to a nearby farm, where they remained safely hidden until the war ended. The possessions were eventually returned to the estate, and are displayed and treasured there today.

During the winter of 1944, one of the coldest in French history, the tides began to turn and the Germans started their retreat across the eastern border. The American Army then took possession of d'Alteville, where soldiers could find relief from arctic winds and snow. Although the property suffered further loss as any remaining furniture was burned for heat, the Americans were forgiven by the family—it was a small price to pay for the successful liberation of their home and country.

After checking into our accommodations, it was finally Ken's turn to head toward his. He would stay with Charles and Marthe at their home in nearby Sarrebourg, located another half-hour away. Ken could hardly contain his excitement during what seemed an endless drive to their town. After traveling along narrow, winding roads slicing through hunter green hills and vales, they came to quaint Sarrebourg and the street where the Kleins lived.

Pulling up to the house, located along a pretty block of tidy homes and yards, Ken could already see Charles approaching him with a huge grin and open arms. Ken's earlier concern that Charles would not recognize him melted away as he opened the car door and heard Charles exclaim, "Kenny! Kenny!" Ken groaned as he pulled his legs out of the vehicle with his hands, and using every bit of strength he could muster, forced his legs into service. As soon as he was upright, he felt the strong embrace of his dear friend, as well as firm kisses planted on his cheeks. Ken returned the affection and greeted Charles heartily in German, calling him "Carl." Ken remarked that he had not seen Charles in a very long time—too long. Then his wife, Marthe, emerged with a shy smile and more hugs and kisses were shared. They had never met, but Ken felt that he knew her well after having exchanged many letters and photographs over the years. He had teased Charles by asking how he had landed such a beautiful wife! Unbelievably, she was now in Ken's arms.

The next hugs were even better than he could have imagined—those of Lisa, Marguerite's great-niece and the Klein's granddaughter, who had helped this reunion become reality. She was even lovelier than her pictures and her big, bright smile warmed Ken's heart. Her husband, Tim, tall and handsome, greeted him as well. Lastly, their children, Vianne, age 7, and Jean, age 5, squeezed Ken tight and offered sweet kisses as well as colorful drawings they had painstakingly created for him. Vianne, with her crystal blue eyes and Jean, with warm, brown eyes, stared up lovingly at Ken, beholding the kind man who had sent them numerous letters and exciting gifts from America for as long as they could remember.

In Ken's mind, the reunion could not have been more perfect. The evening was not yet over, however. Ken grabbed his canes while Charles firmly held his arm and helped him slowly walk to the house, up the stairs, and inside to the family room. It was a comfortable, inviting place with wood paneling, tall shelves with rows and rows of neatly arranged books, and soft leather chairs. Ken's eyes immediately fell upon a painting on the wall—it was of the gateway to the Fénétrange castle. Ken was impressed when he learned that it was skillfully painted by Charles himself. He was also struck by the realization that he was closer than ever to the castle and to *her*.

As soon as Ken sat down, the children appeared before him bearing a bowl heaped with shiny, red cherries. He munched on one as he peered more closely at the drawings they proudly pressed toward him, and then commented enthusiastically on the crayon masterpieces. Jean also presented Ken a small origami boat he had carefully folded, which prompted the storyteller in Ken to recount how he had first come to France—on a big troopship crossing the Atlantic while being stalked by German submarines.

Ken's tale was interrupted by a knock on the door. A reporter and a photographer from the regional newspaper had arrived to interview Ken and to document his return to France.

Questions and cameras flashed toward him, but he kept pace and answered each inquiry like a pro—until the final question. "What memories do you have of Fénétrange?" stopped him in his tracks. Ken choked back tears and no words would follow. It was suddenly quiet. The interview was over.

Charles broke the silence by leaving briefly, then returning a few minutes later with a big smile on his face and something in his hand. He walked over to Ken, and with a grand gesture held the object out to him. Ken's face lit up like a little boy's on Christmas morning. It was Ken's knife from 67 years ago: the one he had given to Charles when they were teens. Ken's sister, Priscilla, had had it engraved with "K.A. Krueger" on the shiny, silver blade and had sent it to him for his birthday while he was in France. Ken was touched that Charles had safeguarded and treasured it these many years.

Charles then proceeded to re-tell the carp story. How proud he was to have caught an enormous fish in the river behind the castle. The carp was over three feet long, a foot tall, and weighed nearly twenty pounds. It was so large that Charles' step-mother stuffed the monster and baked it whole. Ken chimed in that it was the best fish he had ever eaten—an impressive claim considering he had consumed quite a few during his eighty-six years living and fishing in Minnesota, the "Land of 10,000 Lakes."

It was getting late in the evening, but as we had not yet eaten, Marthe quickly prepared a meal for us—an authentic Quiche Lorraine (a specialty named for that region of France), a green salad, bread, and a plate of various cheeses. Before praying and thanking God for His provision, she asked us all to sign her tablecloth. Not only was she a marvelous cook, she was also a phenomenal seamstress. It was a tradition to ask every new dinner guest in her home to write his or her name on the snowy linen. She then expertly embroidered the name with colorful floss to honor and remember each one for many a meal to come.

The family gathered around and happily chatted as we devoured the delicious fare. Ken beamed throughout it all, thinking of how blessed he was to be back there, at long last, surrounded by dear friends and so very near his beloved Marguerite. This was truly another of God's gifts. Greatly enjoying the moment but getting sleepy, we expressed our gratitude, shared hugs, wished them a *bonne nuit*, and then separated for the night.

The next day was Sunday and our team was planning to attend Tim and Lisa's church in nearby Brumath. Charles woke Ken up with the sunrise, and helped him to get a bath before breakfast. On the drive there, Ken shared some amusing stories with Marthe, but suddenly the routine moment became serious. Ken began to speak about something that had been troubling him for quite a long time. He was not sure in his letters to her and Charles whether he had adequately expressed his profound regret at not having returned to Fénétrange and to Marguerite. Although it certainly did not appear to be the case, he worried that they quietly harbored anger toward him for leaving her at the altar and never returning.

Marthe listened carefully, trying to comprehend his English, as he painfully recounted why he never made it back. When he finished, she gazed pensively out the window for several minutes. Then simply, gently she stated, *"C'est pardonné et oublié"* (It is forgiven and forgotten). Ken sighed with tremendous relief at her words. He would not have blamed them, especially Charles, for resenting him. Ken knew that Charles had witnessed his sister's sorrow and humiliation. Hearing that they had forgiven him helped Ken take one more step toward forgiving himself. It also made the trip all the more worthwhile. Another hurdle awaited him at the church, however—Gérard, Marguerite's husband, was going to be worshipping there.

Ken was not quite sure what Gérard had been told about him, or about his relationship with Marguerite. All he knew was what Lisa had revealed while he was at the Klein's—that Charles and Marthe had broken the news of Ken's impending visit a few days before the American soldier's arrival. Gérard, surprisingly, wanted to meet him. (I later learned that Gérard had seen Ken's memoir lying on a coffee table at Charles' house, and Lisa believes he may have even read it. This could explain his curiosity about Ken and his desire to meet him.) Before the trip, Ken's son, Paul, had quipped that if the two men were to meet, there could be literal, hands-on fighting for Delphine. He had grinned as he imagined the two octogenarians punching each other's lights out in the middle of the sermon!

Not knowing what to expect, Ken stepped out of the car and approached the church. The building was set against a brilliant blue sky and surrounded by pink flowers. Ken walked with great effort across a cobblestone square and into the sanctuary. Breathing hard, he plopped into a seat next to Lisa and caught his breath while sweet notes from a piano and flute filled the room. Then the congregation began to sing a tune familiar to Ken. The words sounded especially beautiful in French…

*"Majesté, à lui la majesté
À Jésus soit toute la gloire, puissance et louange…"*

Lisa softly translated the service for Ken. He was surprised by how much it resembled his own church services an ocean away. Unbeknownst to Ken, Gérard sat directly behind him. What was going through his mind? Did he have a clue as to how much Ken had loved Marguerite, though well before Gérard had known her? Did he sense the shame and regret Ken had felt over the years for not having come back for her? Did he know how deeply Ken had grieved her death, though he had not seen her for a lifetime?

Immediately after the service, a petite woman named Lili appeared before Ken with a luminous smile and an envelope in her hand. She asked him if she could read out loud a special letter she had written and had laboriously translated into English for him…

"Dear Mister Ken,

I would like to give you a little testimony. As a grand cousin from Charles and Marguerite, and because I lived not far away from Fénétrange, I had the opportunity to meet them from time to time. I can remember how happy were the long dinners around the table, in a cozy atmosphere with the parents Klein and my cousins. At the time, I was a teenager. I was fourteen years old. I was fascinated by your love story: my cousin Marguerite in love with her handsome American soldier! I was very sad for her when the love story ended.

On one day when I was to Fénétrange, Marguerite offered me a remnant of cloth, from the USA! There were severe restrictions of clothes after the war. I was very happy of this offer! I received in this way a new dress and I was proud to wear it, especially with my friends around me! It was one of a kind. A dressmaker of Fénétrange sewed the dress.

Today, after so long, I am so grateful to meet you and thank you personally for this gift. What a wonderful memory for me! Thanks for coming to Alsace."

Lili

Lili further explained, "The remnant of fabric sent from Ken's mother and offered to me by Margie was a silk. It was light, flowing freely, with a floral pattern of little white flowers on red. This fabric represented a lot to me. It was as a present fallen down from the sky in that time when there was nothing available to buy in the shops. It was a second gift for me. I had a possibility to choose my own style of dress at the same dressmaker who made Margie's wedding dress. At the same time, I had the occasion to meet my lovely cousins: Margie, Charles, and their parents. I did not want to take my dress off anymore—I was very proud of it. I paraded in front of my friends." Ken was moved to know that a simple act of sending fabric meant so much to a young, impressionable girl and that she would remember it all those years later.

Several photos were taken of a beaming Lili, her husband, Jean-Pierre, and Ken. Then it was Gérard's turn. He had been waiting quietly for a moment to formally meet Ken and to share some details of his life with the woman who *was* to have been this stranger's bride. Gérard offered a strong handshake and warm smile, which Ken returned. Gérard was a distinguished-looking gentleman with a head full of wavy, silver hair and sky blue eyes. He had been a successful surveyor who owned his own business, was well-traveled and well-read, and spoke seven languages. Ken could imagine him in his younger days and how Marguerite would have been drawn to him.

Gérard produced several photo albums and proudly pointed to shots of Marguerite, their three daughters, and the many trips they had taken. Ken looked thoughtfully at them and smiled. While he could have felt a twinge of envy, thinking it could have—it should have—been himself in the photos, he honestly was gratified to see her surrounded by her family. To learn she had found a loving husband, with whom she shared a good life, was an answer to Ken's many prayers for her. A man from the church who was listening to all of this nudged Ken and asked, "Are you going to go back (to the U.S.) with a wife from France, *this* time?" Ken replied with a chuckle and a sly smile, "Nah, I'm too old. Besides, it would take too long to train one in!"

We were invited out onto the courtyard to join the family and church members for snacks and beverages, and then to Tim and Lisa's home in Eckwersheim for dinner. After arriving, young Vianne lovingly escorted the slow-moving Ken across the parking lot and up the stairs to her flat. A delicious aroma greeted us as we entered—Lisa's *Baeckeoffe*. This was an Alsatian stew of pork, lamb, beef, leeks, garlic, potatoes, and carrots, which had simmered for hours in an earthenware pot. Ken offered a prayer for the meal, which was followed by a traditional French blessing song where the family sang and heartily pounded their fists on the table.

During dinner, Ken told his well-worn war stories. Not to be outdone, Charles and Gérard began to offer their own tales, which were quite intriguing. It was quickly determined that separate interviews were needed to document the experiences of these former soldiers. After the meal, the family shared priceless memories while looking at old photo albums. Ken was particularly fascinated seeing additional photos of Marguerite with her young family, and then in her later years. Her unforgettable eyes and smile seemed to leap off each page and into his heart.

Time passed quickly and Gérard needed to leave for another family event. Before his departure, we made a request that his story be captured on film and in writing, to which he agreed. Gérard began the interview by stating that he had been among the 130,000 young men in the Alsace and Moselle areas who, from August of 1942 until the end of 1944, were forcibly inducted into the German armed forces. They were assigned to the Wermacht (army), the Luftwaffe (air force), the Kriegsmarine (navy), or the SS (an elite corps controlling the concentration camp system and police forces). Over 3,000 women from that region were also forced into domestic and agricultural work—some into brothels.

Possession of the Alsace area had changed hands many times—five times in just eighty years. During the Franco-Prussian War of 1870-71, Alsace was detached from France and annexed to the German Empire. After the defeat of Germany in WWI, however, Alsace was returned to France under the Treaty of Versailles. The area was under German occupation once again by 1940, not formally annexed this time, but incorporated into the Greater German Reich.

Germany helped herself not only to French resources such as housing, food, and supplies, but also to its young people. Conscripts such as Gérard (and later we learned, Charles) were known as "*les Malgré-Nous*," or Despite Us. This term referred to their having been taken against their will, forced to wear the enemy's uniform and to serve alongside members of an evil regime—one that was doggedly determined to maintain possession of the conscript's beloved country and her people. Resistance was deadly. Those refusing, or later deserting, were hanged or shot to death, and their families were sent to labor or concentration camps. Some men resorted to desperate means of disqualifying themselves from serving with their enemies and possibly against their own citizens by

201

maiming or starving themselves.

Gérard was one of the few Malgré-Nous who made it home alive—more than 30,000 were killed, another 40,000 were injured, and over 10,000 were missing or presumed dead. Those who did make it home after the war were considered to be Nazi sympathizers, or worse yet, traitors by France and the Allies, including the United States.

Debate on the status of these soldiers exists to this day, especially among the families of the victims of German atrocities at places such as Oradour-sur-Glane. In this quiet village of west-central France, thirteen conscripted Alsatian men fought alongside the notorious Waffen-SS. The elite, Das Reich Division of the SS was responsible for the heinous massacre of 642 civilians on June 10, 1944, purported to be a reprisal for suspected Resistance activity among the village people.

During the slaughter, men were forced into barns, pummeled by machine-gun fire aimed at their legs so they would die slowly, covered with fuel, and burned alive. The women and children were forced at gunpoint into a Catholic church and locked inside while the soldiers looted their homes and shops. In an effort to asphyxiate the women and children, gas bombs were set off inside the church. Realizing they had failed, SS soldiers stormed it and began to fire at the innocent victims. Incendiary grenades were then lobbed inside, burning alive those still breathing and writhing on the stone floor. Wood and straw were strewn across the carnage and set on fire.

It is said that the screams were heard over a mile away. For good measure, machine guns were trained outside the church to hammer any escapees. There was just one—a woman who managed to jump out a window and hide in a garden. Then the rest of the town was burned to the ground. One baby was later found crucified and another had been baked in a bread oven.

Former French President Charles de Gaulle decreed that Oradour was never again to be occupied or razed, but preserved as a permanent memorial. The rusted frames of cars, sewing machines, beds, and baby buggies stand just as the enemy left them that day, after five hours of unspeakable terror. Visitors today walk silently among the burnt-out remains of the church, barns, shops, and homes and comprehend all too well what the French suffered at the hands of the Nazis. A sign at the entrance to the village exhorts them: "*Souviens-toi.*" Remember.

Understandably, the extended families of the Oradour tragedy were incensed when one of the thirteen Alsatian men implicated in the horror, who had been given amnesty and released by the French back in 1953, requested a military pension as recently as 1995. This re-ignited passions regarding the Malgré Nous' designation as either war veterans or war criminals. France recently recognized them as ill-fated victims of Nazism, rather than traitors. However, many soldiers are still not considered to be French military veterans, and are often denied compensation in the form of government pensions or disability benefits—even ones in non-combat roles, such as Charles, who was forced to serve as a nurse.

Gérard was assigned as a soldier to the Panzer force (armored tank division) but was soon sent to Hamburg,

Germany, for four months to repair railways, instead. Next, he was transferred to Denmark for six months of training as a telegraph operator, then to Hungary, a member of the Axis powers. He was fortunate in that he was not among the majority of French conscripts who were dispatched to the Russian Front. Those men faced brutal fighting conditions and deplorable Soviet prisoner-of-war camps, if caught by the Russians.

Gérard worked in communications in the small Hungarian town of Tokaj, but was subsequently given a machine gun and forced to fight the Russians. A bullet through the shoulder took him out of commission for two weeks, resulting in his being sent to Budapest. He then went to the eastern-most part of Germany where he remained until the end of the war. Thankfully, he was far from the dreadful Battle of Berlin, which was the final, major Allied offensive of the European Theater of WWII.

Despite knowing the Americans would regard him as a traitor, Gérard planned to give himself up to them, rather than to the Russians, after Germany surrendered. Unfortunately, the Russians arrived first at the city where he lived and he was taken prisoner. He was placed on a train bound for a prison camp specifically for Alsatian men, but he somehow escaped before arriving.

Next, he had to attempt to cross the Russian-controlled part of Austria 300 km (186 miles) by foot while wearing a German uniform—his blond hair and blue eyes made the trek all the more treacherous. Gérard joined hundreds of fellow soldiers walking home to France along *le chemin de troufions,* or soldier's path, who were helped by Austrian citizens—they abhorred the Germans, but had empathy for the French soldiers. He safely made his way to the American zone, surrendered, and waited to be transported to a prison camp. After a three-day interrogation, they simply threw him on a truck to Stuttgart, Germany, and then onto a series of trains back to France.

Gérard's mother, who had four sons in the war, received the best birthday gift that year. She had not heard of her third son's whereabouts for many months and feared the worst. Suspecting this, Gérard wanted to surprise his mother on her special day. He tried very hard to do so, but arrived two days late on June 10, 1945. He felt a bit disappointed but was aware that it was a miracle he was home at all. She, no doubt, was dumbfounded to see him standing at her door. His mother received another belated gift that month: news that her first-born boy, who was taken prisoner in Italy by the Americans while wearing a German uniform, was alive and soon to be released.

Sadly, the family was devastated when the fourth brother never returned. He had been forced to serve in the SS, as Hitler became desperate for more soldiers toward the end of the war, and was stationed in Germany. They never learned what happened to him, until several months later when Gérard met some people who had known his brother. They said he had been hit in the head, was rendered unconscious, and soon died. The incident occurred during a bombing clash along the Siegfried Line (the German equivalent to the Maginot Line) near a town called Linnich, located on the river Rur. After the war ended, it is presumed that the brother was one of several SS men whose unclaimed, unnamed corpses lay unburied for months. The Nazis had destroyed all of the soldiers' military documents, so that the soldiers could not be identified. They had also destroyed a dam in the area, inundating the land with water, so there was no place to bury the dead. Gérard was told that six months later, his brother was finally laid to rest, along with other nameless SS personnel, in numerous tombs for the unknown.

When asked how it felt as a Frenchman to be forced to be complicit with the enemy, Gérard responded with resignation that his uncles were French, fighting on the German side during the First World War as was he during the Second. It was simply the way of life back then. When asked how it felt to meet the man who had been engaged to his wife, he replied that in his mind, Ken's visit was no longer about Marguerite. It was simply about the brotherhood of two men who had both survived war.

Ken understood and appreciated Gérard's perspective. In Ken's mind, though, his having returned there was still about Marguerite and his promise to her. Now it was time for what Ken both delighted in and dreaded—going to Marguerite's grave.

Chapter Four

Enfin

The tears came swiftly and silently. No sooner had he stepped through the cemetery gates in the Alsatian town of Molsheim than he felt that all-too-familiar sting behind his eyes. Ken had hoped to remain composed for as long as possible. Sorrow simply could not be restrained, however. His blurred vision made it even harder to make his way down the path, but he kept trudging along using a cane in each hand for balance. It was eerily quiet for late afternoon. The only sound was the crunch of his heavy shoes on gravel as he shuffled toward the grave, though an occasional chirp of a bird, darting across the spring sky, punctuated the relative stillness.

Ken clutched four bright pink roses in one hand—a modest offering for his long-lost love—as he moved closer to her grave. Had he glanced up he would have taken in quite a beautiful site. The cemeteries in France are very different from any Ken had ever seen. Rather than simple headstones resting on a grassy lawn as in Minnesota, each French gravesite was unique and interesting. The grounds, surrounded by an old brick wall, were divided into distinct plots by rectangular ledges measuring about a foot high. Many plots had built-in planters along their edges with a rainbow of flowers and greenery cascading to the ground. Around the sites, large plantings burst forth with fragrant purple lavender or pink, showy blossoms, while shrubs and evergreens filled in the gaps between the graves.

The front three-quarters of each plot were covered with various materials such as crushed rock, soil, or a slab of shiny granite, plus more flowers. Around the ledge were placed special mementos—awards, tributes, eulogies, poetry, or photos encased by stone frames to personalize each loved one's final resting place. At the back quarter of some tombs, a large, ornate headstone stood listing one or more names. (Often, several family members were interred in the same plot.) On others, a tall cross was erected, with the names and dates of the deceased engraved on an adjacent piece of granite, like that of Marguerite.

Ken's breathing was labored and his brow was beaded with sweat by the time he neared the grave. This was due in part to exertion but also to elation: it was the closest he had been to her in over sixty-seven years. He stopped before the tomb, and with his canes, steadied his legs which were shaking with the searing pain of bone rubbing on bone. The late-afternoon sun illuminated his face, highlighting deep wrinkles glistening with tears as he glanced up to see the massive cross looming over the place where she lay buried. He looked to either side of the tomb and noticed the well-tended, scarlet flowers growing in tidy rows. Finally, casting his eyes downward he saw what he had dreaded most: the name "Marguerite NEY (nee KLEIN) 1925-1999" in gold, raised lettering staring up at him.

Ken paused to catch his breath and calm his throbbing heart. There they were—stark letters and numbers. They coldly confirmed what he knew in his mind: that under that sparkling stone, in a silk-lined coffin, rested his beloved Margie. He envisioned her lying there, still and quiet, just as he had done when he heard of her death. Ken attempted to push the image out of his mind. Nevertheless, that image was quickly replaced by the other one that had plagued him most of his life—the last time he had seen Margie alive. He had stopped to look back at her while heading toward the train station. To this day, he was haunted by those remarkable blue eyes dripping with raindrops and tears. He could still feel her cold, wet hands fiercely clinging to his sides. He could still hear her final words as she pleaded with him to make a promise they both feared would never come to pass.

Ken bent down as low as his arthritic legs and back would allow, and tenderly placed the roses on her grave. He desperately desired to kneel down even further, to be as close as possible to Marguerite, but knew he did not possess the strength to pull himself upright. Ken struggled to stand, and then closed his eyes, praying silently. After quite some time, he whispered "amen," raised his head, and began to speak the words he had waited a lifetime to utter.

"Hi, Margie. I never thought I'd see this day. I-I'm so sorry I hurt you. I never intended to hurt you. Please forgive me for all the pain I caused."

His voice weakened and failed as heavy sobs overwhelmed him. They were indeed composed of the bitterest tears for words left unsaid and deeds left undone. His cries echoed briefly across the tops of the tombstones, then were absorbed by the centuries-old walls of the cemetery. Raw anguish was paired with profound relief, that at long last, he had said those words —"I'm sorry." He had completed the deed—he had returned.

Gradually, his trembling shoulders began to calm. Leaning on just one cane, Ken brushed his cheeks with the back of his hand while clearing his throat. His voice recovered, low and a bit stronger, allowing him to continue his somewhat random thoughts…

"I'll always remember the good times we had together. You sure were a honey!"

"I know you're in Heaven—no pain, no sorrow."

"Thanks, I know you've forgiven me."

As Ken paused again, a verse came to mind, Philippians 4:6-7: "Do not be anxious about anything, but in everything, by prayer and petition, with thanksgiving, present your requests to God. And the peace which transcends all understanding, will guard your hearts and your minds in Christ Jesus." Ken needed that peace desperately. Only God could provide it. He knew what he must do—pray with thanksgiving, express his request, and trust in God's power to heal his heart and mind.

Ken bowed his head and thanked the Lord for His faithfulness in the past. He expressed gratitude for having known Margie when he was a young soldier, and for the privilege of knowing her family now. Ken's request was simple—"Lord, I know you have forgiven me—please help me forgive myself." At that moment, Ken chose to trust that, once and for all, his sin was forgiven and forgotten by the One who had come to die for that sin. The sense of peace that God promised began to wash over him. Thankful beyond measure, Ken stood motionless, praising his Savior. After several minutes, Ken raised his head, turned his attention back to Margie, and began to offer a brief, final farewell.

"All I can say is goodbye for now. Someday we will see each other—forever."

He began to turn away, wincing in pain for having stood so long. He heard the sound of footsteps approaching and was joined by Charles, Marthe, Tim, and Lisa. They offered a wheelchair for him to rest in and joined him in prayer. Then, with a few leftover tears and heavy sighs, Ken said his last words to her…"I never stopped loving you."

With the sun grazing the horizon, it was time to leave. He grabbed the wheels of his chair, turned, and slowly began to push himself back up the gravel path toward the exit. This time… he did not look back at her.

Chapter Five

Le Temps s'Arrête

Early the next morning, as he gazed down the brick road that wound into the medieval town of Fénétrange, Ken marveled at how little the town had changed since the war. Quaint shops, restaurants, and flats, all with clay roofs, colorful shutters, and tan stucco walls lined the narrow streets. Several churches and buildings, topped with enchanting witch's hat towers, looked much as they had years ago. He recognized the bakery and the butcher shop, which had the same family names on their doors. These staples of the community had been passed down to children and grandchildren—even to great-great-great grandchildren.

Beyond the large archway through which Ken had driven his jeep untold times, Castle Fénétrange still stood. Much to Ken's dismay, however, the Castle (also known as le Château de Fénétrange) had undergone a major renovation and looked very little like its old self. The interior had been gutted and refigured to offer space for shops, offices, and apartments. Gone were the tall tree in front and the deep stone well standing in its shade. The well had provided fresh, cool water to a soldier weary of the brackish liquid in his canteen. Gone were the tall piles of chopped wood that would keep a castle cozy, or at least habitable, all winter. Thankfully, the basic design and character of the façade had been preserved. Its cream-colored plaster, gray and red stone trim around the windows and doors, and characteristic brick-red tile roof had been faithfully restored.

We met with Charles as well as Christine and Laurent, the reporter and photographer, respectively, who had first interviewed Ken at Charles' and Marthe's home in Sarrebourg. They were continuing to document the soldier's return to Fénétrange for the regional newspaper, *Le Républicain Lorraine*. The next step was to inquire whether our group could see the house in which Marguerite and her family had lived, and where Ken had stayed and fallen in love. The house had stood behind one of the large sets of wooden doors of the Château. The little bell Ken had always rung to gain entrance was no longer there. Ken wondered about the fate of the house.

Our team and the newspaper staff waited expectantly outside the doors, after having knocked several times. Minutes later, a young woman with an inquisitive look on her face, slowly opened one of the heavy doors. Much to everyone's great relief, the old home was still there overlooking the Saar River—what a gift to behold it again. Ken was not only relieved that it had not been razed or replaced, but he was thrilled that it appeared exactly as it had in 1945. Charles had to offer a detailed explanation to the wary woman as to why we were there before she, somewhat begrudgingly, allowed us to enter the courtyard and to film on the premises.

Ken found himself walking into the very place he had dreamed of night after night. Glancing up, he could not believe he was actually standing below the window of the room where he had slept. White lace curtains covered the glass, and wooden shutters with bottle green paint framed the window, just as he remembered. Imagining what lay beyond the window, he thought of the bed with clean sheets, a warm duvet, and a feather pillow—heaven for an exhausted young soldier. Beyond the bedroom door was a narrow hallway. There, Margie had stood shivering in his arms, fresh from her bath, on what should have been their wedding night. How he had been able to contain his emotions and not simply sweep her into his room or carry her away into the night was beyond him.

Turning his attention to the yard, he scanned its familiar contours. It still held a small, unkempt vegetable garden on one side, but no longer a pen for a pig. Pink and white geraniums spilled from pots, and tall, red rose bushes grew wildly along the walls of the shed where Margie's dad had once made Calvados. Ken noticed one thing missing, though—there was not one purple delphinium in sight.

He walked to the edge of the small yard and gazed down at the narrow river flowing gently below a terraced hill. On the opposite bank was a pretty park crisscrossed by streamlets whose contents gushed into the main flow. The bubbling water was quickly swallowed up by the current and quietly sent along its way downstream. Ken was instantly transported back in time. He and Marguerite are gliding down the river together again in the duckboat built by Charles and his father. She turns back at Ken and smiles, while playfully splashing him a little with her paddle. He returns the smile with a twinkle in his eye and threatens to douse her. Instead, he continues a strong, steady stroke of the oar. Ken feels like the luckiest guy in the whole world. Next, he is sitting with her on a blanket at the edge of the river. They are holding hands while watching the sun sink in the sky. As he leans over to press his lips on hers…

Ken was startled from his reverie by a request for photos. He was directed to sit on a dilapidated wooden bench, which seemed to be held together by nothing more than layer upon layer of peeling paint. While examining its rusted wrought iron sides and splintered, narrow slats, he wondered whether it would even hold him. He suddenly recognized it as the very same bench he had sat upon many times with Margie! It certainly looked all of its many years, and then some. No one would guess that lots of good smooching had once taken place upon it.

As Ken sat in the noonday sun with his dear friend Charles at his side, he was overwhelmed with thankfulness to the Lord for that special moment. Once again he felt close to Margie and to himself as a young man in love for the first time. No longer was there an aching feeling of regret—only tender memories of her. The photographer took myriad pictures of Ken, Charles, and me (one of which landed on the front page of the French newspaper) while Ken softly spoke with stunning detail about his time there as if it were yesterday.

Knowing how much Ken would love to see the inside of the house, Charles did his best to convince the woman, a tenant, to allow the old soldier inside. She was not at all interested in having anyone enter, even for a quick peek. It was decided that perhaps the owners could be contacted and an appeal made for a brief visit another day, since he had come so very far for this once-in-a-lifetime experience. Our entourage left, with some reluctance, after having thanked the tenant warmly. We were glad to have at least seen the exterior, the yard, and the river.

We began to stroll through the town as Ken pointed out places and events he recalled, such as the time he walked through Fénétrange in a German uniform he had confiscated from a Nazi warehouse. Although he had an army buddy walking on either side of him for protection, Ken was quite fortunate not to have been captured or shot by the Allies who controlled the area.

As Ken was wheeled down one street that ran along the river, he began to sense something familiar about the area. He believed the American XV Corps Headquarters was nearby—a place with which he was very familiar, since he had always retrieved his messages there before heading out for a delivery. Searching for landmarks to guide him, he suddenly declared it should be past the trees ahead, and sure enough, a huge building came into view. Ken was stunned that it was standing there. The Headquarters, a handsome school before the war, appeared to be long-deserted. Thick slabs of paint were hanging off its sides. Tangled webs of vines and grasses sealed the doors, creating a massive spider's lair of sorts. A view through broken lower windows revealed abandoned scraps of equipment and furniture planted in mud and decorated with weeds. Ken wondered why it had never been torn down or rebuilt. It simply stood there, forlorn and forsaken, at the edge of town.

It was time to meet with our contact in Fénétrange, Monsieur Marc-André Kuhn, the town pharmacist and local historian. His great-grandfather had established the town pharmacy in 1877. Marc-André owned and ran the business, like his father and grandfather before him. He also headed le Syndicat d'Initiative, a nonprofit organization that helped document and preserve the rich culture and history of Fénétrange. Marc-André and his wife, Sonia, had graciously made special arrangements for Ken's visit and offered exclusive access to several venues of interest to Ken and our team.

Our first stop was le Musée, a small but fascinating museum located in an old cottage near the Collegiate Church. The museum contained artifacts highlighting Fénétrange's medieval past. It also offered displays depicting French home life, and the work of artisans in the 19th and 20th centuries. One room was particularly interesting to Ken—that of the town *charron*, or wheelwright. That person was none other than Marguerite's father, Frédéric. Ken was intrigued to see the very tools he had used, as well as several wheels made with his own hands. A photo on the wall made Ken laugh—it was of Frédéric looking rather glum, as usual. Ken said he could not help thinking of him as that "sauer-kraut."

Next, our group was invited to the Kuhn home for refreshments and to meet Marc-André's aunt, Madame Marie-Thérèse Kuhn-Wendling. She was just a year younger than Marguerite, and still remembered details of the day that Ken and Marguerite were to be married —details that would once again stab Ken's heart. We entered the home, a few doors down from the pharmacy, through a narrow hallway that emptied into a quintessential French *salle á manger* or dining room. The charming room held a large table surrounded by cabinets and racks displaying a collection of china and local pottery. Beautiful dinnerware and bakeware pieces were hand-painted with earthy colors reflecting the Alsatian countryside.

We appreciated the offer of orange juice and *les sablés,* French butter cookies, while we got acquainted. It was a challenge to keep up with the conversation—a spirited mix of French and English—with our limited proficiency in their language. We understood exactly what was being discussed, though, as the topic turned to that fateful day in November when Ken and Margie were to be married. Much to everyone's deep regret, Mme. Kuhn-Wendling verified what I only imagined had happened: that Ken had, quite literally, left Margie standing at the altar.

Mme. Kuhn-Wendling recalled that the church bells were clanging to herald the joyous event, as the young bride-to-be waited in the church that Saturday morning. Marguerite was surrounded by family and friends while the townsfolk chatted cheerfully outside, ready to greet the young couple after the ceremony. (I later learned that the first stop for a couple would have been the town hall where a civil ceremony takes place, followed by a religious benediction at the church.)

Marguerite must have stood there for quite some time in her finery, while holding flowers in her trembling hands—first with a heady sense of anticipation, but then with mild annoyance at his being late. As the minutes passed with no groom to be seen, anxiety must have swelled within. Was something wrong? Did he have the day or time mixed up? Did his jeep break down or was it in an accident? Was he hurt…or worse? Or did he simply get "cold feet?" Had he changed his mind altogether?

No, she knew that her "Kenny" loved her deeply and that he was a man of his word. After all, he had proposed and had sent for a ring from America. He had told his family and army officials about the wedding. His mother was simply ecstatic and could not wait to meet her new daughter-in-law, while his buddies were almost as happy as the groom-to-be. Ken had helped to plan the wedding, had arranged the honeymoon, and had received time off from his army duties. Everything was set. So where was he?

Anxiety would give way to fear, then to denial, then anger. At some point, the awful realization that he was not coming at all would force her to tearfully, reluctantly head out the door, push her way through the crowd, and run home to an empty bed. Her panoply of emotions would not be completed quite yet, however. It would be topped off with burning humiliation. Before this horrible day had even arrived, some townsfolk had whispered behind Margie's back that Ken would never marry her. They had claimed that he was just like all the other soldiers who had moved through town—soldiers who wooed the girls and promised them the moon—then left without as much as a goodbye.

Marguerite heard the rumors and had fiercely defended Ken, saying he was not at all like the others. Her retorts only served to invite further speculation and ridicule. Later, she would become the object of pity when the predictions came true. With their suspicions about Ken confirmed, several people in the village outright laughed at Margie. Mme. Kuhn-Wendling reported that no one in the community, other than Margie's parents and a few relatives, ever knew that Ken had finally made it to Fénétrange, and that he had still desperately desired to marry her. Nor did they ever know why he had not come for the wedding, choosing to believe the worst about Ken. Marguerite left the town in despair and disgrace, and wandered inconsolably for months.

Ken felt compelled to tell Mme. Kuhn-Wendling, in his own words, exactly what had happened. He explained that although he immediately applied for the pass after they had planned the wedding, it was not until several weeks later that Ken learned the request was denied. By then, it was too late to get a message to Margie before the wedding day. Crestfallen, Ken took comfort in knowing he had told her firmly that he may not make it back on that particular date. He was at the mercy of the Army, so she and the family would need to wait until they heard from him before proceeding with their plans. Ken went on to say how he had fought for the pass but lost. He had no recourse but to return to Fénétrange two weeks later after the pass was suddenly granted. Ken literally ran to her from the train station and pleaded with Margie's father to allow them to marry. Frédéric was adamant that there would be no wedding.

Ken then shared his experience of going AWOL for a day to say goodbye to his first love, perhaps for the last time. He recalled how he was on his way back to the United States after the war ended and had, on impulse, hopped off his troop train to catch a train to Sarrebourg and then to Fénétrange. Ken stated this was the one and only time he was ever absent without leave. He also told of his anguish at seeing the printed signs enticing soldiers to re-enlist as he was leaving the area for the second time, and being conflicted as to which way to turn.

Mme. Kuhn-Wendling, hearing the desperation in his voice, gently told him that she understood that it was not his fault and assured him that all was forgiven. The events had happened very long ago. To the people of Fénétrange, it was now simply an old wedding story, no doubt one among many of that era. Mme. Kuhn-Wendling also said, with a coy smile, that had *she* been the one engaged to him, she would have forgiven him immediately and married him then and there! This clearly delighted Ken, but more importantly, he was thankful and relieved that the townsfolk understood and held no resentment.

It was time to move on, as there was still much of Fénétrange waiting to be seen again. After lunch at an Alsatian restaurant, the newspaper folks went on to another story while the four of us pressed on to two places etched into Ken's mind: the meadow and the train station. We drove to an area just outside and above Fénétrange, which offered a breathtaking overview of the town. Stepping out of the car, we were captivated by a vast, green meadow spread out before us. Decorating the valley beyond were rolling hills, stately trees, meandering rivers, red-roofed cottages, and white church steeples with the Vosges Mountains serving as a verdant backdrop.

Though glorious to behold for all of us, for Ken there was a special significance to this place. He had met Margie in the very same meadow, on more than one occasion, after having returned to Fénétrange by train during a break from his army duties. The fresh, cool grass provided the perfect spot to enjoy a picnic lunch and precious time alone. As Ken took in the landscape, it was not difficult to bring her back to mind: dark, wavy hair framing smooth, pink cheeks; blue eyes fringed with dark lashes; the faint scent of lavender; her cotton dress billowing in the wind; grass-stained toes; and warm, tender lips.

The Fénétrange train station, which had been his frequent destination and desire during the last year of the war, was just down the road. Ken was anxious to see it again, although he had been warned not to venture there during his visit by a well-meaning old-timer in town—gypsies were illegally camped on the land. Some lived in the long-abandoned station with their families despite having no running water or electricity. More respectfully referred to as the *Roma* today, these unwelcome immigrants from Romania or Bulgaria were feared not only as pickpockets, petty thieves, and beggars, but rumor had it that they ate people!

Taking our chances, we drove toward the nearby station and stopped at some railroad tracks leading to it. We were amazed to see the year "1941" still clearly emblazoned on the side of the rusty iron rails. Following the track, past the tall grass that had not seen a scythe in decades, our eyes widened when we came upon the weathered building with the word FÉNÉTRANGE, faded yet visible, on its front.

Desiring to get some close-up shots of the station, we drove up to two men working on a near-skeleton of a vehicle. It appeared as if they were dismantling the heap, perhaps in an effort to salvage its metal. Along the dirt road, shabby trailers were lined up, like those at a county carnival used for hawking cotton candy and corn dogs. One wondered whether the vagabonds traveled around in them selling their wares or lived in them—maybe both.

Believing it was wise to be courteous, we stopped the car and rolled down the window to ask the men whether they minded our taking a few photos. It was strangely quiet, except for the noise of dogs yapping and the clanking of the men's tools. There was neither sight nor sound of children, despite several trikes and toys strewn around the area, along with assorted debris. Apparently comprehending our request, the men replied, "*Mais, non, bien sur.*" Then from grease-smeared faces, bright smiles emerged. We smiled back, expressed our thanks, and pulled up next to the station.

The four of us had an eerie sense that tiny eyes were peering down at us from the station's upper floor. The windows were covered from the inside with scraps of colored paper, obscuring our ability to confirm our suspicions. I scrambled out of the vehicle and tried to catch a perfect shot of the station while quickly exploring the grounds. It was gratifying to see the place with my own eyes—Ken had described it to me so many times that I felt as if I had been there.

Ken stared quietly at the stucco structure for some time, then pulled himself out of the car and gradually approached it.

He was fairly incredulous that the old building was intact and that he was in its presence once more. It was in remarkably good shape, considering it had not felt the rumbling of a train pulling up to its platform for many, many years. Looking up at the Fénétrange sign, Ken's pulse raced, much as it had years ago upon arriving back to where his girl would be waiting for him, day after day. How he wished she were waiting there still.

Chapter Six

Les Souvenirs

Marguerite was gone. Nothing could change that. Ken felt deeply blessed, however, to have received the gift of time with her brother. Ken looked forward to reminiscing with Charles and learning more about the Klein family history. He also hoped Charles could shed light on what had happened that day he was to have married Marguerite. An interview was scheduled at Lisa's home so Charles, Marthe, and Lisa could share their memories and reflections.

Charles began by saying that he was born on August 23, 1927, in the same large house where his sister had been born, just down the road from the Fénétrange Castle. Regrettably, his mother, Marie, died in September when Charles was only three weeks old and Marguerite was a toddler. Marie had developed a relentless fever after giving birth. A post-partum infection was thought to be responsible for her death, but no one really knew in those days.

Marguerite was sent to live in a village, not far from Fénétrange, called Harskirchen. Lina, her father's sister, along with Lina's husband and three children, raised young Marguerite while Charles remained in Fénétrange. A local woman volunteered to act as a wet nurse to feed tiny Charles.

227

She had recently given birth to her own son, Auguste, and generously stepped forward to provide nourishment for both babies. The boys were called *les frères du lait* or "milk brothers," and remain special friends to this day. (True "bosom buddies," *n'est-ce pas?*)

Six months later, Charles' father married his sister-in-law, Pauline. (Days before she died, Marie requested that her sister marry Frédéric.) That arrangement worked well for everyone. Frédéric had companionship and someone to help him raise the children; Pauline had been unable to have children of her own, so this enabled her to experience motherhood; and the children were brought up in a loving home, as Marie had desperately desired.

Charles holds tender memories of being reunited with Marguerite and growing up together. His eyes were filled with tears, and his voice was pinched with emotion, as he recalled special moments with his sister. When they were ages two and four, he told of being cold or frightened at night. Charles would sneak into Marguerite's warm bed and snuggle with her, only to find himself back in his own bed the next morning, having been carried there by his stepmother. Charles and Marguerite had great fun playing together as children and were very close. When they were older, Charles said that he often came to his big sister's rescue when bullies would tease her. He never understood why they did so—she was always very kind to everyone. He characterized his sister as a "pearl," possessing fine, rare qualities.

Charles also talked about his father. Besides having been an excellent wheelwright, he was a talented mechanic and had built an entire car by himself. Frédéric was a hard worker who did whatever was necessary to care for his family during the turbulent days of occupation and war. Although their strict, uncompromising father was a man of few words, the children knew they were dearly loved and grew to have a staunch respect for his authority.

Along with Gérard and fellow sixteen and seventeen-year-old boys from Alsace, Charles was coerced to join the failing German war effort. He did not wish to be found hanging from a tree or lamp post—the chastisement for those deemed traitors by the SS. German boys, known as Hitler Youth, were forced to fight at even younger ages—some as young as twelve years old. Charles was sent to a camp for army training in Bayreuth, Germany, and was taught nursing skills. The last week before the war ended, he and his fellow conscripts were commanded to go to Berlin by foot, a 221-mile hike. This represented a foolish and futile attempt to stop Stalin's assault on the German capital.

Charles had a German comrade in the camp whose Christian parents lived on a farm near Bayreuth. Knowing they would be headed for a suicide mission in Berlin, Charles and his friend miraculously escaped from their unit, and disappeared into the dark night. They bolted barefoot to the family's farm, donned civilian clothing, and hid in the hayloft. The boy's parents had placed their own lives at grave risk in concealing them, since the village was swarming with Nazi soldiers and sympathizers. The very next day, the line of fire approached the area: Russians were streaming in from the east and south, while the Americans were poised sixty miles west of Berlin.

As fighting raged around them, the two young men lay motionless under the hay, and the family huddled in the farmhouse. Three long, terrifying days later, the mortar fire died down and American GIs appeared in the village. The German soldiers had been routed and Charles, as a Frenchman, was free to return to France. He was thankful to be transported by a U.S. military jeep to an assembly camp, and then by plane to Nancy, France. Finally, Charles was issued official discharge papers and boarded a train to Fénétrange.

On May 8, 1945, Charles returned home. All the town bells were ringing triumphantly at the news that the war in Europe was over—Hitler was dead by his own hand. With his demise and Berlin having fallen, the Nazis had finally, mercifully been defeated. Not knowing that the armistice with Germany had been signed, Charles believed the chimes were ringing for him! He hopped off the train and hurried toward the castle to surprise his family. They had not seen their son for nearly a year, and did not know whether he was even alive. Several young children recognized Charles when he arrived at the station and scurried ahead to the Klein home with the good news. The family immediately dropped what they were doing and, with disbelief tinged with hope, ran toward the station. A tearful reunion ensued as they met and clutched each other in sheer joy and relief. The interminable years of death and destruction were at an end. The Kleins praised God for the safe return of their only son and prayed for restoration of their beloved country.

Charles remembers meeting Ken after the American soldier had returned to Fénétrange from duty in Austria.

Language was no hindrance to the budding friendship. Charles proudly stated that he had won first prize in English, and that Ken had picked up French after having lived there for two years, so they could communicate well enough. The young men canoed, fished, and hiked together when Ken was in town, and they became good pals. One day, before Charles left to continue his education at a school in Sarrebourg, Marguerite revealed the good news that she and Ken were even *closer* pals and were actually engaged to be married. Charles had been a bit surprised by that revelation, yet very pleased. Ken was soon to be not only his dear friend or *copain*, but also his brother-in-law.

It was not to be, of course. Charles witnessed his sister's torment as the minutes, and then the hours, ticked by with no groom. As a loving brother, Charles certainly felt great compassion for his sister. As a fellow soldier, he also guessed what Ken's predicament was: a pass to Fénétrange must not have been issued by the American Army. Short of going AWOL, the young private had no option but to wait for permission to leave. Charles did not blame Ken in the least for not making it to the wedding, yet he agonized over how to help Marguerite understand. Charles knew that his father never would.

Charles was already back attending high school when Ken finally got the pass and returned to Fénétrange two weeks later. Ken was gone again, this time for good, when Charles visited the family the following week. Not knowing what had transpired while Ken was there, Charles had hoped that, by some miracle, the marriage had taken place after all. As soon as he entered the house, Charles knew something had gone terribly wrong. Marguerite was inconsolable, his father was enraged, and his step-mother was utterly silent.

Charles soon learned why. Frédéric had not only refused to allow them to marry after Ken had arrived in Fénétrange, he had also forbidden their becoming husband and wife—ever. Marguerite pleaded with her father to re-schedule the wedding, but she could not change his mind. Charles tried his best to comfort his sister, and to convince her that she had no choice but to accept their father's decision. He had learned long ago that no meant no.

In looking back, Charles said he understands his father's frame of mind. Frédéric had lost his own father when he was a small boy. As a young husband, he had lost his first wife. His only son had been taken captive for nearly a year. His only daughter was determined to marry an American. She would leave her home and family, sail across the ocean, and begin a new life. He may never see Marguerite again. If the young couple were to live in France, or even across the border in Germany, their union might have been somewhat tolerable to Frédéric. If they were to live in the United States, their union would be unthinkable. Far too much had been lost already to the family, to the town, and to the country during the harrowing years of war—another loss simply could not be sustained.

Charles also sensed that his father's pride had been irreparably damaged. Earlier, Frédéric had agreed to allow his daughter to marry this American soldier, albeit begrudgingly. He had also overseen the preparations for the wedding, and was scraping together enough francs to provide a nice celebration for them—the only thing missing was the groom. Now, all he had to show for his benevolence was a hysterical daughter, bills for a reception that never took place, and a town full of people mocking them. The final straw must have been when Ken and Marguerite asked him for permission to try it all over again two weeks later!

On the other hand, it was difficult for Charles to see his sister in so much pain, and even more heart-rending to hear her express unwavering confidence in Ken. She believed with all her heart that, even if her fiancé were to sail to the States alone, he would come back for her as he had vowed. In a few months she would be twenty-one anyway, and could legally marry without her father's permission. While waiting for Ken, she hoped she could persuade her father to allow the marriage one day as she would prefer his blessing. That day never came. A year later, Ken would reveal in a final letter to her that there was someone else in his life. He would not be coming back to marry Marguerite after all.

Marthe recalls this time well. Marguerite was still dealing with a shattered heart when Marthe and Charles began dating. She had noticed the handsome, young Charles back in 1947 when they took the same train to school each day in Sarrebourg. She had been impressed that he carried a violin with him, and that he was studying to be a teacher. At first it seemed he did not notice her, but then Charles began to leave little notes on her desk. That gesture captured her attention, and eventually her affections. Charles and Marthe were married in Strasbourg in 1948. For thirteen years, the young couple lived with their three children in an apartment above the school where Charles taught. The school was located in the small town of Postroff, about 4 kilometers from Fénétrange. Next, they moved back to Sarrebourg where they live to this day.

When Marthe first met Marguerite, they bonded instantly and were much like sisters. Marthe said Marguerite was always well-dressed, preferring simple styles and quality materials in her clothing and shoes, and was also well-coiffed. She enjoyed serving in her church choir, hiking in the Vosges Mountains, cooking, and sewing. Marthe remembered the handsome blue chambray shirt that Marguerite made for Ken out of the cloth he had confiscated from the German warehouse.

Marguerite possessed an easygoing, bubbly personality and loved to laugh and talk. These qualities endeared her to the gentle, unassuming Marthe. Ken was often the topic of conversation. During those moments, Marguerite's face would fall and her voice would soften as she shared memories of her "Kenny." She couldn't help wondering aloud… what if? What if he had made it to the altar in time? What if her father had allowed them to marry two weeks later? What if he had returned for her as he had promised?

Marguerite never dated again—not until she met Gérard in Paris several years later. Marguerite was working as an *au pair* with the same family for whom her mother had served as a cook, and her aunt as a governess, a generation earlier. She heard through her family that a relative named Gérard was visiting Paris and she arranged to have lunch with him. They soon learned that they had more in common initially than most people. Gérard was her great, great, great cousin (they shared a great-grandmother). Love quickly blossomed during their Sunday walks together, and it was not long before they were engaged to be married. From that time on, Marguerite never spoke about Ken to Marthe. She and Gérard went on to have a wonderful, fulfilling life together. They married, had three daughters, enjoyed wealth, and traveled to exotic locales such as Egypt and Kenya.

Marguerite died on February 22, 1999, at the age of 73, one day before Gérard's 75th birthday. Our team was surprised to learn that Marguerite had not died of cancer, as Ken had been told previously in a letter from the family (though she did suffer from the disease). Gérard explained that she was involved in a serious car accident—one so grievous that she had to be cut out of the vehicle. She recovered, but years later Marguerite was informed that she needed a knee and hip replacement as a result of her previous injuries. Before the surgery was performed, her doctors discovered that she had a lack of white blood cells in her body, a condition called neutropenia. This disorder raises the risk of bacterial infections, including life-threatening ones such as sepsis, and compromises healing after injury or surgery. She was advised to delay the procedure until her immune system could be improved, but Marguerite insisted on going ahead with the operation. Despite the risks, it was performed and was deemed successful.

Grand-niece, Lisa, remembers the last time she saw Marguerite. It was while she was in the hospital recovering from the surgery. Her great-aunt was sad, and a bit embarrassed that people had to see her in that pale and disheveled state. Lisa was encouraged, though, to hear excitement in her aunt's voice and to see a spark in her lavender blue eyes when the doctors gave her permission to go home for a while. Marguerite was eager to be back in her own bed, and to be able to prepare one of her delicious meals of Alsatian Wild Rabbit once she regained her strength.

After returning to her flat in Strasbourg and cooking dinner with her daughters, Marguerite declared that it was the best meal she ever had. It was also one of her last. She became gravely ill from septicemia (bacteria in the blood), as doctors had warned, and then died from septic shock. Marguerite had earnestly prayed about going home, and God indeed answered. He chose to take her to her eternal one this time.

As a teenager, Lisa loved visiting her grandma, Marthe, and hearing her relate the sad tale of the handsome American soldier who *almost* married her great-aunt. The story stoked the imagination of a romantic young lady to the point where she felt the pain of the seemingly star-crossed lovers as if it were her own. Lisa would pore over a map of the world to locate Minnesota, and try to envision Ken and his life in the United States. She dreamed of meeting him one day, and could not have been more astonished when in 2005, over a decade later, she received a phone call from her Grandpa Charles. He told her, with much emotion in his voice, that a letter was sent to him from Ken's brother, Russell, on Ken's behalf. This man was no teenage fantasy—he was real!

Letters from Ken, himself, followed. Lisa had the pleasure of translating them for her grandparents, and then writing back to Ken. She and her husband, Tim, had lived in Boston, Massachusetts, for several years, so they could read, write, and speak both languages well. Charles and Marthe knew some English also, but it had been ages since they had been given an opportunity to use it. Marthe began to work on her English skills by corresponding with Ken, and gradually was able to assume the task.

As Lisa worked on translating those first letters between Ken and the Kleins, the reality of this "cruel destiny" weighed upon and broke her heart once more. Ken had begun to search for his Margie decades after their final words to each other, only to learn that Marguerite had already left this earth. She would never know that he had fulfilled his promise—not in this life, anyway. At the same time, Lisa rejoiced when she read that Ken was a believer in Jesus Christ, as was she since the age of twelve. Ken wrote that he had been thinking of and praying for Marguerite and her family ever since he had left France. Lisa was amazed that someone so far away had been faithfully talking with God about them. It began to dawn on her that many of the answers to prayer she had witnessed throughout her life were God's answers to Ken's prayers as well. Several times each week for over sixty years, Ken, often joined by his wife, Mae, had asked God to save, protect, and guide Marguerite and each member of her extended family. The Bible states that the "prayer of a righteous man is powerful and effective" (James 5:16b). Lisa sensed that very power working in her life and in the hearts of her loved ones, as Ken obeyed God's command to pray without ceasing. He knew that God uses our prayers as instruments to accomplish His purposes and sovereign plan.

Lisa went on to say that she had thought about Ken quite often as she grew up, but never dared to mention his name to anyone again, especially to her great-aunt. She always sensed a residual sadness in Marguerite, and guessed that she could never completely get him out of her heart. Lisa never learned that Ken had made a solemn promise to return one day—had she known that, Marguerite's sorrow might have been better understood as the bitter disappointment it truly was. Even today, Lisa believes that although Marguerite was blessed with a wonderful husband and a fulfilling life, she never quite forgot her first love—because *no one* ever really forgets.

Chapter Seven

Peut-être Pas

The next day, similar to the time at l'Arc de Triomphe in Paris, Ken received an unexpected gift. Their Fénétrange host, Marc-André, announced that not only had he arranged a meeting for Ken with the town's mayor, but that a special ceremony had been planned to recognize Ken for his role in helping liberate France. That morning he dressed in a new shirt, sweater, and slacks; placed his "magic" hat over his carefully-combed hair; and splashed a bit of cologne on his neck. Later, he would not regret the extra effort he had made to look his best.

We all arrived outside *la mairie* or town hall, bright and early. The tan brick building with turquoise blue trim had not changed since Ken had last been there—even the bulletin board that had displayed Ken and Marguerite's engagement decree was still there, announcing the happy news of modern-day couples. Ken was wheeled into the entry and greeted warmly by people in French period costumes and by military officials. After shaking hands he craned his neck toward a vaulted ceiling. Ken seriously doubted that he could make it up the steep, winding staircase to the third floor, where various dignitaries and townsfolk awaited him. One of our team members asked an official whether the upstairs was wheelchair-accessible. With a twinkle in his eye, he proclaimed, "*Mais, pas de problème, Monsieur!*" Suddenly, three burly Frenchmen appeared out of nowhere. They grabbed Ken, wheelchair and all, and effortlessly hoisted him up three, long flights, much to our amazement.

Whisked into a room filled with cameras flashing and people applauding, Ken felt like a movie star and attempted to take it all in. Peering past the crowd, he saw an elegant space whose walls were covered with paintings depicting the well-known Fénétrange Castle. One table offered refreshments of cake, orange juice, and champagne while another table was covered by a cloth with an American flag design. French flags were held by decorated veterans from the UNC, an association for veterans' affairs, and from Le Souvenir Français, a group which conserves the memory of those who have died for France and maintains memorials to them. Reporters stood ready with their notepads, while soldiers and civilians waited patiently for the festivities to begin.

Several more people were wearing medieval costumes, including men in black robes and hats holding a *voulge*—a menacing-looking weapon that resembled a hatchet mounted on a long shaft. The men portrayed *les veilleurs de nuit,* or night watchmen, who made their rounds of the town from 9:00 p.m. until 3:00 a.m. beginning in the 14th century and concluding in the 19th. They also wore an animal horn around their necks to blow as a warning of fire or other impending danger. (This tradition continues as today's watchmen walk the streets of Fénétrange during the summer months and early autumn.)

Suddenly, a tall, attractive woman with long legs and high heels emerged from the crowd. She approached Ken, knelt down beside the wheelchair, and proceeded to give him a nice, firm kiss on each cheek. Holding his hand and gazing deeply into his eyes, which were dancing with delight, the woman introduced herself as Madame Nicole Horvath—the presiding Mayor of Fénétrange. Ken laughed and exclaimed, "Wow! That's the first time I've ever been kissed by a mayor!"

She continued to speak with Ken warmly in English. Sensing an entrée and thankful he had taken the time to dress up, Ken began to grin, wink, and flirt with her unashamedly. Then, perhaps thinking better of it, he started to play matchmaker on behalf of his bachelor son, Paul, and suggested that he and the mayor would make a great couple. Madame Horvath graciously played along and chatted with Ken for some time, while cameras continued to flash and click.

Then it was time for more serious business. A highly-decorated gentleman in a plaid sports coat walked up to Ken and presented him with two awards: a baseball cap adorned with the emblem of the UNC, as well as a lapel pin with the same insignia. The UNC supports men and women who have served in the French military, as well as veterans' widows and war orphans. The representative, M. Charles Huber, spoke a few words of gratitude, affixed the pin on Ken's collar, and then saluted him. Ken was quite touched to become an honorary member of that organization.

Next, the mayor offered Ken special gifts—a beautiful

book of nature photography and two signed prints of turn-of-
the-century Fénétrange. This was followed by a toast to Ken,
refreshments, and an opportunity for people to speak with him.
Ken enjoyed meeting the friendly people of Fénétrange and
was fascinated to converse with two who remembered him
back in 1945. They each had played a role in his would-be
wedding! One was the UNC representative, M. Huber who
stated that his father's family had owned the local *boulangerie*,
or bakery, since 1684, and that his father had actually baked
the cake for Ken and Margie's wedding. Afterward, a woman
named Madame Jeanne Muller-Nonnenmacher shyly
approached him and said she was the seamstress who had made
Margie's wedding dress. She recalled that Marguerite had been
completely confident that Ken would be there for the big day.
Mme. Muller-Nonnenmacher said that she had gently
cautioned, "*Peut-être pas.*" Perhaps not.

When asked what the dress had looked like, she
explained that it was actually a skirted suit. Cloth fabric was
difficult to find during the war, due to trade restrictions and
blockades, forced shutdowns of factories by the occupiers,
rationing, and German requisition (confiscation). The French
women had to make do with whatever was available. In
Fénétrange, the only thing one could purchase was wool.
Margie's bridal "gown" consisted of a light grey wool jacket
and skirt. (We learned that Marguerite wore this suit rather
than the traditional pale-blue dress her mother had made for
her.) This was probably not the wedding attire of her dreams.
However, one supposes it was of little consequence to a young

bride-to-be who could not wait to become Mrs. Kenneth Alden Krueger.

Soon the festivities were over. The mayor, the officials, and the guests offered their goodbyes and went back to their everyday lives, having respectfully paused to meet this living "legend." Ken felt honored yet humbled by their attention. He also sensed nagging anxiety, as this was his final day in Fénétrange, and there was one thing he must do before leaving.

The mighty trio of men re-appeared, swooped Ken back down the stairs, deposited him on the sidewalk, and disappeared before anyone could even thank them. Then the mayor and her entourage marched past him. She turned back to look at Ken and they blew each other kisses. Ken then began to roll himself, instinctively, to where he felt drawn—the place where they would have become one in the Lord.

Tears once again began to intrude, even before he had gotten himself past the wrought iron gates and through the front door of the modest Lutheran church. He stopped to rest in the cool, quiet, empty chapel. Before him stretched an aisle, flanked with worn wooden pews, which led to an altar. Sunlight streamed through two tall stained glass windows behind the altar, illuminating the colorful depiction of Jesus' birth, death, resurrection, and second coming. The light also set the altar aglow, highlighting its elements—a large Bible, a crucifix, candles, and flowers. Looking down on Ken was the symbol of the All-Seeing Eye of God embedded in the ceiling, and behind him loomed a large, ornate pipe organ.

Ken moaned as he struggled to raise himself up from the chair, and with the assistance of his canes, he began to inch his way up the aisle. Ken was determined to stand where Margie had that day—exactly where they would have become husband and wife. After several minutes of shuffling, he arrived at the altar and slid the cap off his head. He was in physical pain, yet he knew it paled in comparison to the emotional pain Marguerite had experienced as she waited and waited for him to arrive. He felt so near, yet so very far from her. With his head bowed and shoulders hunched, Ken stood motionless and mute. He prayed for a long time, and then began to speak softly, as if she were there. What was expressed is known only to Ken.

A piercing pain in his legs began to overwhelm his thoughts. With a Herculean effort, he retreated down the aisle and tumbled into the wheelchair. Ken slowly wheeled himself back out into the noonday sun. The wooden door of the church creaked as it closed behind him. It shut with a thud that briefly echoed through the chapel, then died away.

That evening, we enjoyed another excellent meal at the home of Charles and Marthe, followed by a heavyhearted farewell. Ken had always loved the Kleins. Having now spent time with them, he felt an even more intense bond and held even deeper affection for them all. He considered them part of his family. Lisa expressed similar thoughts—that no matter what had happened between Ken and her great-aunt, the Minnesota soldier was a part of their family, and would always be thought of as such.

Their time together was more than Ken ever dreamed. It had gone by all too quickly though, as do most good moments. They all silently wondered whether they would ever meet again. Charles and Marthe had never been to America and did not feel able to travel that far. Lisa and Tim were busy with their young children, careers, and a possible move. Ken hoped to return to France in a few years to promote the updated memoir, but he put his destiny in the Lord's mighty hands. "For I know the plans I have for you," declares the LORD, "plans to prosper you and not to harm you. Plans to give you hope and a future" (Jeremiah 29:11).

Before beginning the final days of our trip, which would be spent in the Normandy area, we drove further east. We planned to explore the lush Vosges Mountains, the picturesque villages of Alsace, and the sophisticated city of Strasbourg, which straddles the border of France and Germany. One definitely sees the German influence in eastern France in everything from the names of towns, to the architecture, to the food: the best of both cultures in one unforgettable region.

The first night, we were booked at a small hotel in the middle of one of the many vineyards in the area. Tidy rows of grapevines covered the rolling foothills. The grape leaves drank in the warm sun while the roots feasted on the rich soil. A charming German restaurant adjacent to the hotel served huge platters heaped with fat homemade sausages, ham, potatoes, and sauerkraut, followed by sweet apple strudel. After dinner, looking up toward the mountains, one could see the twinkling lights of tiny villages sprinkled across the hillside. A large glowing light dwarfed the smaller ones: it illuminated the outline of a massive building standing sentinel over the valley.

Curious about that light we had seen, our team set out

the next morning to discover its source. We learned it was from le Château d'Andlau, a 13ᵗʰ century castle ruins made of local granite blocks and sitting on a narrow outcrop near Gertwiller, France. The castle is being restored by a group called la Fédération du Club Vosgien, which maintains and waymarks footpaths and hiking trails. Having come upon the trail leading to the castle, we decided to take Ken on an adventure. At first, it was relatively easy going for Greg and Troy to push Ken through the thick woods. However, the path became increasingly steep and rocky as they moved closer to the castle. Eventually, they were forced to stop. Ken was weary by this point, too, and asked to be left in the woods to rest. He pointed out, with a gleam in his eye, that he had his walking canes to protect him from vicious animals. We were apprehensive about this being a wise idea, but Ken insisted we finish the trek to the castle, which was about a mile away. Having continued on the trail, the three of us were rewarded with a fascinating look at the medieval structure and a breathtaking view, while Ken snoozed safely in the middle of a sunny glade.

On our final day in the east of France, we explored impossibly charming Alsatian towns. Their brightly-painted, half-timbered homes and shops welcomed visitors with window boxes overflowing with masses of flowers. We attended a festival in a small town in Germany, just across the border, and then relaxed in a peaceful park along the Rhine. Ken thought back to the last time he had stepped foot in Germany. The war was over, but not some of its hardships. The American Army was running low on rations. Its soldiers were getting hungry—very hungry. At one time they were so desperate that Ken and his friends were forced to dig with their bare hands through spent garden plots to glean rutabagas and turnips. Their stomachs gnawing, the men would pull up the abandoned vegetables, brush off the dirt, and stuff them into their mouths raw.

Once, they stumbled upon a hapless, small deer. It was shot, prepared by the army cook, and swiftly polished off by the ravenous troops. Another time near Salzburg, Austria, Ken and his buddies seized an entire 40-pound crate of C-rations, consisting of cans of meat and beans, meat and potato hash, or meat and vegetable stew. They made a soup of sorts by mixing it all with water, then heating it with a blow torch, and pouring the concoction into their canteens for a "gourmet" meal.

As we made our way to Strasbourg, Ken was overjoyed to find an authentic Sherman tank of the 2nd French Armored Division on display in a small memorial park. The tank, provided by the Americans, had possibly been part of the Allied breakthrough of the German defenses near Avranches, France, after D-Day. It had apparently churned its way across France to the German border, and commanded by French General Philippe Leclerc, was instrumental in his victory in reclaiming Strasbourg. Ken had delivered messages to that division nearly every day during the war, but had not seen any of the tanks since then, other than in photographs printed in WWII books. Its history was acknowledged on a plaque that read, "In memory of the soldiers of the 2nd Armored Division killed for the liberation of Strasbourg—November 23, 1944."

Our time in Strasbourg was a wonderful way to end this part of the journey, although it certainly left a desire to see and do more in this enchanting city, perhaps on a return trip. Strasbourg is the principal city and capital of the Alsace region, and is the official seat of the European Union's legislative body, the 766-member Parliament. The city has a vital port and is rich with art, museums, parks, restaurants, medieval architecture, and the graceful Rive Ill. The river winds its way through the town and under several pedestrian bridges. Dominating the city is the impressive Cathédrale Notre Dame de Strasbourg, a magnificent gothic church made of pink sandstone, which is the tallest medieval structure in Europe. It was built between 1190 and 1493 and stands on the site of an ancient Roman temple.

We finished the day in Strasbourg with dinner under the stars at one of the many outdoor cafés in the square adjacent to the Cathedral. It was a captivating sight, as day gave way to evening and the square came to life with people strolling, chatting, laughing, shopping, and eating, all under the shadow of the colossal church tower. As Ken bowed and shared a mealtime prayer, he thanked God for His abundant grace toward the four of us. We had experienced safe travels; the beauty of nature; meeting wonderful people; and priceless time with Marguerite's family. God had yet another gift to bestow upon Ken, though. He would receive it where his French adventure had begun so many years ago—near the shores of Omaha Beach.

Chapter Eight

Leurs Vies pour Les Nôtres

      After a seven-hour drive back across France and a night in Rouen, of Jean d'Arc fame, we continued to a small town in the countryside. Cerisy-la-Salle, located just twenty miles from the Normandy Coast, would serve as our base as Ken was reunited with his past. Checking into l'Hôtel Goffêtre, we were warmly greeted by our French hosts, Guy and Nadine, who had been looking forward to having a real American veteran stay at their lovely *chambre d'hôte*.

      Early the next day, we drove to Sainte-Mère-Église. This village was occupied by German forces from 1940 until 1944, and it was the first French town liberated by air during the D-Day invasion. Its liberators, the American 82nd and 101st Airborne divisions, were assigned one of the most difficult tasks of the initial phase of the invasion, called "Operation Overlord"—they were ordered to jump into the darkest hours of the morning, arriving five hours before the Allies were scheduled to land along the coast.

      Over four hundred C-47s, carrying thousands of paratroopers left England around midnight. The men were dropped in the vicinity of the westernmost Allied landing beach, code named, "Utah," around 1:30 a.m. of June 6, 1944. Unfortunately, many were shot on the way down, or were drowned in the fields. Nazi troops had flooded the area for just that purpose. The men who survived were the first Allies to step foot in occupied France. Despite several snags, or perhaps because of them (poor weather created much confusion on both sides), the village was free from Nazi tyranny by 4:30 in the morning. The establishment of a beachhead along the Normandy coast had begun.

One such snag was quite literal. Private John Steele, with the 82nd Airborne, famously landed on a church roof in Sainte-Mère-Église, and was caught by his parachute cables on the church spire. He feigned death while hanging above the fierce combat on the streets below. Two hours later, the Germans cut him free after discovering he had been "playing 'possum," and made him a prisoner. Steele managed to escape with the help of his army buddies and returned to the same town to continue the battle. The young private was instrumental in defeating the enemy, despite the excruciating pain of a foot injury caused by exploding antiaircraft shells, or flak, when he had descended into the dark. Private Steele would recover and then go on to help liberate a key city in the Netherlands and participate in the Battle of the Bulge, among other assignments. He later received the Bronze Star for his bravery and a Purple Heart for the injuries he had endured while in combat.

An Airborne Museum in Sainte-Mère-Église is dedicated to the memory of all members of the 82nd and 101st divisions. The museum holds over 4,500 artifacts from WWII, including objects used by the paratroopers on the night of June 5-6. One highlight is an actual Douglas C-47 Skytrain, which had transported paratroopers during the D-Day drop. To further commemorate the valiant efforts of the airborne soldiers, a reenactment is held each year around the anniversary of D-Day. More than 700 paratroopers from Britain, the United States, and ironically, Germany, were scheduled to drop in a large field near the village of La Fière (literally "the proud"), west of Sainte-Mère-Église that very morning we visited.

Several battles with the Nazis had occurred at La Fière Bridge, which straddles the Merderet River. Possession of the bridge was critical to both sides. The Allies needed to gain control of the bridge and the adjacent causeways. (The causeways were the only paths available to move troops, vehicles, and supplies from the beaches, across marshes and lowlands, and then further inland.) The Germans needed to stop the Allied progression across France. Brutal fighting took place around the bridge over many days, but the Americans emerged the victors. They repelled the German forces and held their position, allowing the Allies to continue the liberation of Normandy, and eventually the entire country.

Ken was greatly looking forward to the sight of the sky filled with hundreds of jumpers. They would represent the 13,000 who had heroically plunged into the abyss the morning of D-Day, and possibly into the hands of the enemy, during those early hours of the invasion. Thousands of spectators had already gathered in the vicinity by the time we arrived, as had ominous charcoal rainclouds. Visibility was poor, but Ken hoped the drop could still be made.

As he was wheeled through the crowd, people made way and stared at his "magic" hat. When they recognized Ken as an American veteran, they began to smile while offering their hand and conveying their gratitude. Several asked for his autograph or requested a photograph with him. Once again, Ken was surprised and humbled by their attention and responded warmly with smiles, winks, and handshakes.

Inevitably, the pendulous clouds gave way to showers and people popped open colorful umbrellas or scampered beneath trees. While our foursome was pondering where to find shelter, an American soldier from the 101st Airborne Division, one of the most highly-decorated units of the Army, approached Ken and asked whether he would like to get out of the rain. Ken grinned and nodded gratefully. Immediately, similar to the time in Fénétrange, three burly men from the 101st swooped him up in his wheelchair, pushed aside some barricades, carried him down a long, gravel road leading to the parachute drop zone, and deftly deposited him under a large tent covering a stage. The soldiers offered a salute and then quickly disappeared into the drizzle.

Ken looked around him and was amazed to see that he had been plopped, once again, right into the middle of a sea of dignitaries. He found himself surrounded by veterans from the 101st and 82nd Airborne Divisions and other units, active service members, and special guests who had been invited to that 67th anniversary of D-Day. Ken was incredulous that he, a Signal Corps veteran, was spontaneously included in the Airborne's festivities. He was even given a prime seat for observing the paratroopers, which no doubt had long been reserved for one of their members. The tent was crammed with people attempting to stay dry, but two veteran soldiers, one from Britain and one from France, made room for Ken and his wheelchair next to theirs. The old soldiers, who had rows and rows of colorful medals adorning their jackets, greeted Ken and then returned to chatting softly to each other while the crowd waited for the big event.

Sitting quietly and observing the eclectic crowd, Ken was suddenly the recipient of more unexpected attention. He was surrounded by curious attendees who grabbed his hand, thanked him, requested a photo or autograph, and asked him questions in various languages. While enjoying the exchange, it was announced that, due to heavy fog, the drop had to be cancelled. There was a collective sigh, but everyone understood that it was too dangerous to jump, let alone fly a plane. The disappointed crowd reluctantly began to disperse. Ken and the team had just started walking back up the road when the three strong soldiers appeared again, picked Ken up, and whisked him over the bumpy gravel road to a paved one. He had never received such "service" in the States!

The rain had begun to slow enough that they could see what else was happening in the area. There was a display of vintage American military jeeps, trucks, motorcycles, and other vehicles lined up in a re-creation of an encampment. The vehicles had been abandoned after the war, but were now beautifully restored down to the tiniest detail. French reenactors portrayed American troops, nurses, and WAC members (Women's Army Corps). They looked very much the part in their impeccably detailed outfits and hairstyles. It was heartening to see young people, through role-play, honoring and remembering the men and women who gave so much for the freedom enjoyed in France today.

"We must remember your good work. God bless you and thank you," said one reenactor with tears in his eyes. He shared that his grandfather had lived in Normandy at the time of D-Day, and was dying. Ken responded by taking his hand and assuring the young man that he would be praying for his grandfather. He offered hope in this verse, Isaiah 41:10: "So do not fear, for I am with you; do not be dismayed, for I am your God. I will strengthen you and help you; I will uphold you with my righteous right hand." The man nodded in appreciation and returned to his duties.

We left Ken alone for a few minutes so we could explore "Camp Overlord." Upon our return, he was surrounded again by a small crowd—they asked about his service; had him sign their books, hats, and shirts; and even interviewed him on film for a British television show. Ken spoke with a gentleman who had served as a paratrooper with the British Regiment, telling him about his time in Fénétrange with the mayor. Then, Ken was tickled to meet a man, from his home state, who wore a Minnesota Twins baseball cap and now lives in Paris. Next, an Army general approached him and shared how he had begun his military career in the Signal Corps. Ken especially enjoyed meeting the young children, who unabashedly wrapped their little arms around his neck, reminding him of his own precious great-grandkids back home.

Ken was bemused by all the adulation—he had no delusions of grandeur. He was simply thankful that he could play a role in liberating France, and acknowledged that he was just one of the 16.1 million American men and women who served during WWII, who did not feel they had done anything heroic or exceptional. They simply did what their country called them to do, what they were trained to do, and what their hearts told them was the right thing to do.

Another event soon began: a formal ceremony to unveil a memorial dedicated to the medics of the 505th Parachute Infantry Regiment of the 82nd Airborne. After landing, those paratroopers had installed first aid stations and surgical facilities within the first hours of the Allied assault. Medical personnel cared for their own wounded, as well as civilians and even enemies who were injured. The medics put themselves at great risk: they were unarmed and often had to dodge vicious cross-fire to rescue soldiers. Their job entailed moving the wounded away from combat lines, transporting them to first aid stations, providing treatment, and then eventually evacuating patients to medical boats or planes back to England, or in some cases, to the United States.

The ceremony began with four American soldiers carrying both the American and 82nd Airborne flags into La Fière Memorial Park, accompanied by a military band. A long row of U.S. officials and service members stood next to their French counterparts. A large statue of "Iron Mike"—a symbolic soldier whose nickname refers to someone who is unusually brave, tough, and inspiring—rose into the bright blue sky. The monument pays tribute to the many paratroopers who lost their lives in Normandy: over 2,500 on D-Day alone.

A speech was given by an 82nd Airborne member, who

noted how the courageous soldiers of D-Day had changed the course of the world. Despite overwhelming odds, men who were ordinary became extraordinary. He thanked the French people for remembering the Allied sacrifices, and recognized the Army medics who had played such a vital role in saving lives. The speech was followed by the laying of a dozen red, white, and blue floral wreathes near a plaque which reads, "To pass on the memory, to remind us that today, we live in peace, freedom, and dignity because others gave their lives for us." The national anthems of America and France were played, followed by "Taps." After the ceremony, the band continued to play as they marched out of the park and right past Ken. He was surprised and touched to see the name of the band on the large bass drum—"Luftwaffen Musikkorps4—Berlin."

While Ken was observing the ceremony, Greg sneaked away and returned with a special treat for Ken. It was an authentic Army jeep, very similar to the one that had been his constant companion for two years in Europe. The female reenactor at the helm smiled brightly and invited Ken aboard. He was jubilant in having the chance to sit in one again, though it was a challenge to get him from the wheelchair into the passenger seat. "I used to hop right in them like nothin'," lamented Ken. At the same time, haunting memories of the tense hours spent gripping the steering wheel while driving fearfully in the dark under the threat of sniper fire, treacherous land mines, and immense tank traps gave him a shiver up his spine.

Bitter weather had exacerbated that relentless fear of the unknown. The winter of 1944-45 was one of the coldest on record. Ken learned to shift the gears of the jeep with his feet while sitting on his hands or stuffing them inside his coat in an attempt to keep his fingers from literally freezing. Looking out over the dashboard, he remembered how he had to tilt the windshield in a certain position so that the piano wire the Germans had cleverly strung across the roads would not slice off his head. Despite the bittersweet thoughts running through his mind, Ken appreciated a moment to step back in time, and sincerely thanked the young lady for her kindness in bringing the jeep to him.

With the ceremony ending, we moved on to one last stop for the day—the nearby town of Sainte-Marie-du-Mont, believed to be the first town liberated by the troops landing by sea. A re-creation of a U.S. field camp was set up around a medieval stone church. The tall bell tower of the church was a focal point of the tiny town, and was used to great effect by the Nazis as an observation tower. When the four of us arrived, the village was buzzing with people acting out various roles, giving one a sense of the sights, sounds, and activities of that epochal time. A parade of men dressed as Allied soldiers marched triumphantly down the street, while the rumbling of tanks, trucks, and half-tracks in the distance was pierced by the screaming sirens of resurrected emergency vehicles. Other people portrayed American soldiers, medics, nurses, and assorted personnel as well as French police officers, soldiers, and townsfolk. A sea of green tents, vehicles, and soldiers enacting army life filled the church yard and beckoned visitors to walk within.

True to form, as Ken was wheeled through the camp, he

was encompassed by reenactors who briefly broke character to greet him, ask questions, or get an autograph or picture with a WWII veteran. One man was particularly interested in meeting Ken—he was the French version of him! He had been portraying an American Signal Corps soldier for over twenty years, but had yet to meet a real live GI who had been there as a youth. The irony of being an American veteran in France and speaking to a Frenchman pretending to be an American was not lost on Ken!

The soldier the man was representing would have traveled across France and delivered messages as Ken did, but not through mail dispatches. He was acting as a radio operator who transmitted vital communications with a radio set-up in his jeep. The reenactor invited Ken to check out his vehicle and equipment, and then with great flourish, handed him his pride and joy: an authentic Thompson submachine gun. Ken was thrilled to be able to hold one again. It was the first time in decades. Although he had, miraculously, never been forced to pull its trigger during the war, he had been thankful for the sense of security it provided during his many encounters with the enemy. Ken was deeply impressed by the dedication and attention to detail the French reenactors exhibited, not to mention the outlay for the artifacts they possessed. The "tommy" gun alone would cost $25,000-$45,000 in the United States. Add to that the purchase and maintenance of the jeep and equipment, travel expenses, time off work and more, and you have quite an investment in keeping alive the memories of those who gave their lives for yours.

It was quite a day. Ken was honored more than he felt

he ever deserved. The next day, however, Ken would be the recipient of one final gift—one too wonderful to have ever existed in a dream.

Chapter Nine

Le Chemin Parfait de Dieu

Much to his wonder, Ken had unwittingly become a celebrity, of sorts. This became even more evident while we were strolling through the walled city of le Mont-Saint-Michel, named for the patron saint of many a French king. The city is built on a granite outcrop situated in the flats of a river estuary between the Normandy and Brittany regions of northwestern France. A breathtaking medieval abbey rises majestically from the center of the small tidal island. Along a narrow cobblestone lane winding up to the Abbey, charming shops, hotels, and cafés beckon its three million yearly visitors to step inside.

Walking by one restaurant, we noticed a nicely-dressed gentleman standing casually against the wall with his arms crossed. We were startled when he began to grin and declared, "Ah, Monsieur Krueger. *Bienvenue*! Would you be interested in dining with us this evening?" He acted as if he were awaiting the veteran's arrival. We Americans looked quizzically at each other and asked how in the world he knew who Ken was. The gentleman chuckled and replied that he had read several stories about him and had seen his photograph in various newspapers. He explained that Ken was becoming well-known in France!

Smiling in amazement, we took him up on the offer of a meal. We were shown to the best table in the house and provided complementary beverages and hors d'oeuvres. A delicious dinner was peppered by questions about the beautiful "Delphine," which were posed by the owner and the servers. The staff was curious to learn more about the young lady who had driven an American man, while in his twilight years, to travel thousands of miles across the ocean—only to say goodbye. They not only agreed that she must have been quite an exceptional girl, but also asserted that all French women possessed *un je ne sais quoi*—an indefinable yet charming, captivating quality. Ken concurred, "*sans doute!*"

The last day of Ken's journey was to begin with a final interview. Sébastien Brêteau, a reporter with the regional newspaper, *Ouest France,* had also heard about Ken's compelling story from newspapers in the east of France. He had contacted me through another journalist who had documented the visit. We made an arrangement to meet at the visitor's center of the Normandy American Cemetery in Colleville-sur-Mer, which overlooks Omaha Beach.

Monsieur Brêteau would gather information for two articles on Ken—one highlighting his promise to return to France, and one requesting help in finding another young lady, Yvette Delacotte. The reader will recall in the first part of this book how twelve-year-old Yvette had befriended Ken and sold him green beans while he was delivering messages in the Normandy area. They had corresponded with each other for several months in 1944-45, even after his unit had moved on.

Ken often wondered what had happened to her after the war—
if she had, indeed, survived it.

    While driving to the cemetery along the bluffs of lanky,
wind-swept grass dotted with clumps of yellow flowering
bushes, one could see the menacing-looking remains of several
German bunkers attempting to hide in the dense weeds. Vast,
deep bomb craters carpeted with emerald green grass punctured
the land. Gazing across the bluffs, Ken marveled at the
turquoise water of the sea and cornflower blue of the sky.

    He was even more intrigued to see remnants of the
"Mulberry Harbors" in the distance—two temporary, floating
artificial ports that were personally ordered into production by
British Prime Minister Sir Winston Churchill. All of the useful
French harbors were occupied and heavily fortified by the
Germans, so in one of the greatest engineering feats of the war,
ten-mile-long, flexible roadways were manufactured in
England by the Corps of Royal Engineers. The pieces were
then towed by tugboat across the Channel, and assembled off
the coast of Normandy. The roadways were made to float on
concrete pontoons that led to the beach, thereby speeding up
the movement of troops, vehicles, weapons, and supplies
crucial for Allied victory.

    Despite one harbor at Omaha being decimated by a
storm just a couple of weeks after completion, a second one
further east, on British-liberated Gold Beach, was still
serviceable. It was known as Port Winston and was installed
near Arromanches. Seven thousand tons of cargo was
transported from ship to shore each day until the Allies could
capture and secure the French ports. Ten months after D-Day,

2.5 million men, 500,000 vehicles, and 4 tons of supplies had been successfully delivered via the fabricated roadways. Today, all that remains are enormous rectangular blocks of crumbling concrete decorated with barnacles, plus rusted remains of scuttled ships used to create breakwaters. They seem to march across the horizon in a glorious, victorious procession.

We came to a road that cut through the bluff and went down to a beach with golden sand, appropriately named La Plage de Sables d'Or, better known as codename "Omaha." Ken could not wait to get out of the car and step once again on the strand where he had begun the journey of a lifetime. As he struggled to pull himself out of the vehicle, the scorching pain in his legs returned. It was nearly forgotten in anticipation of that moment, however. He steadied his wobbly limbs and began to walk across the kelp wrack and to the smooth, unblemished sand beyond the high-tide line.

There were a few other people walking silently, reverently along the coast. Lost in their own thoughts, they took no notice of Ken. This was no place for conversation, or frolicking in the surf, or picnicking on the beach. It was a killing field. Ken stopped to catch his breath and realized how peaceful it was there. The rhythmic rolling of the waves was somehow soothing, and had long ago washed the sand clean of the blood spilled by 2,000 young men. It was hard now to envision the hellish reality that had greeted our advancing troops—the chaos, smoke, explosions, red-stained water, and limp bodies floating toward shore. How could such terror have existed where such tranquility now reigns?

He looked to the tall ridge behind him and wondered what it had been like for the soldiers attempting to scale it. Gazing beyond the ridge, he smiled at what he had seen on his first day in Normandy back in July of 1944—the red, white, and blue of the American flag thrashing in the wind. The very colors are a testament to soldiers like Ken, who served and to those who continue to serve our country today. Red signifies valor and the willingness to sacrifice. Blue stands for vigilance and justice. White represents pure intentions and high ideals. The ideal of securing God-given freedom for all people spurred those men to slog through icy, choppy water; to crawl across 300 yards of open beach littered with barbed wire, mines, beach obstacles, and the bloodied corpses of their buddies; and to claw their way up 100-foot tall hills under the rain of Nazi machine gun, artillery and mortar fire at the rate of 100,000 rounds per minute.

Ken paused to say a brief prayer of praise to God for those intrepid heroes all along the Normandy coast and across Europe who had reclaimed liberty with their very lives. He thought of a quote he once heard by Thomas Campbell, "The patriot's blood is the seed of Freedom's tree." The old soldier turned and began to hobble back to the car. His already red-rimmed eyes started to fill as he was handed a small glass bottle holding the flaxen sand of Omaha, which I had scooped up as a memento for Ken. He cherishes it to this day.

Ken sat in silence as we drove up the winding road toward the American cemetery. He was struck by the beauty of a canopy of tall hardwood and evergreen trees, and the precisely-manicured lawns that stretch to the sea. We stopped

briefly at an overlook on top of the ridge above the beach.
From that vantage point, it seemed even more improbable that
anyone could climb up the bluffs while under torrents of
gunfire and survive the onslaught. As we were pondering the
events of that day, a team of French reporters approached Ken,
requested permission to film him, and began to ask about his
involvement in the war. He shared a few memories of his
experience coming across the beach, and soon a small group
gathered around him, listening intently.

Soon we had to excuse ourselves, as it was time for
Ken's scheduled interview in the visitor's center. The center is
the entry point for the memorial grounds and contains
interpretive exhibits to inform guests about the 1944 military
campaigns, which led to Allied victory less than a year after the
beginning of "Operation Overlord." The exhibit also highlights
the personal experiences of soldiers through journals, letters,
photographs, and artifacts, offering a face and life story to
some of the thousands of names on the marble headstones.

Ken met with the reporter and began to share his story,
which appeared the next day in the regional newspaper. In a
footnote to his article on Ken and Yvette Delacotte, Monsieur
Brêteau asked readers to contact him with any information
about the family. We would later learn from a great-niece that
Yvette had indeed survived, had served in the French Army in
Paris for many years, and now lived in a nursing home 40 km
southeast of the capital. Ken would have been thrilled to
correspond with her again, but efforts to contact her have not
been successful.

As the interview wrapped up, Ken noticed a quote, the

first of many within the cemetery, engraved on a nearby wall. It affirms the true intent of the invasion, lest anyone hint that the United States entered the war for any imperial aspirations—

"If ever proof were needed that we fought for a cause and not for conquest, it could be found in these cemeteries. Here was our only conquest: all we asked was enough soil in which to bury our gallant dead."

General Mark W. Clark
Chairman, American Battle Monuments Commission, 1969-1984

It was enough—172 acres provided by the French people for the 9,387 souls to be buried by their families in the foreign soil on which they had died. Each grave is marked with the name, regiment, and date of death of a soldier who had perished on D-Day, or during the ensuing operations: all except the 307 unknown soldiers whose headstones are noted simply with, "Here rests in honored glory a comrade in arms known but to God." It is staggering to look out across the sea of alabaster crosses and Stars of David that appear to go on into infinity. It is sobering to see how they all face toward the west—toward home.

Desiring to see the rest of the grounds, Ken was escorted first to the memorial, featuring a 22-foot bronze statue called, "The Spirit of an American Youth Rising from the Waves." The magnificent form of a young man reaches dramatically for Heaven. Encircling the granite base of the monument is the inscription: "Mine eyes have seen the glory of the coming of the Lord." Upon the stone floor, whose pebbles come from the landing beach below, was laid a large floral display in the form of our flag. It was made of red, white and blue carnations. The memorial is flanked by a semicircular limestone colonnade. Carved across the lintel is the inscription: "This embattled shore, portal of freedom, is forever hallowed by the ideals, the valor, and the sacrifices of our fellow countrymen."

Across from the memorial, at the base of a central mall, is a large reflecting pool where water lilies grow—symbolizing renewal of life. Along one side were placed over a dozen beautiful floral displays presented by dignitaries of various French towns. They were bursting with the same red, white, and blue color scheme as that of the French and American flags and bore ribbons that read, "We have not forgotten." Behind the memorial, one sees the sobering Walls of the Missing, where 1,557 names are inscribed of soldiers assigned to the Normandy area who were never seen again. Some may have been swallowed by the sea, or mingled with others in a mass grave. Others may be lying alone deep beneath a farmer's field, or hidden in a tangled hedgerow. The names represent just a fraction of those still unaccounted for from the entire war— over 73,000 individuals.

At the other end of the mall, which bisects the grave plots, is a circular chapel. Engraved on the exterior is this tribute: "These endured all and gave all that justice among nations might prevail and that mankind might enjoy freedom and inherit peace." Inside, a mosaic ceiling depicts America saying farewell to her soldiers, and a grateful France placing a wreath upon America's dead. The inscription offers God's comfort and assurance in the midst of grief—"I give unto them eternal life and they shall never perish."

It was getting quite late in the afternoon and the grounds were closing soon. However, Ken required a quick snooze and was wheeled to a quiet corner beneath the unusual truncated trees gracing the mall. (The trees, trimmed straight across the top and down the sides, represent the lives of young men cut short in war.) His brief nap enabled the rest of us to walk the grounds before the two flags on the mall would be lowered for the day—those of the United States and France waving high atop poles near the graves. A brief ceremony is performed at 5:30 each evening. This is followed by a bugler playing the haunting notes of "Taps," which, perhaps unbeknownst to many, was given these original lyrics:

Day is done, gone the sun
From the lakes, from the hills, from the sky
All is well, safely rest
God is nigh.

Fading light dims the sight
And a star gems the sky, gleaming bright
From afar, drawing near
Falls the night.

Thanks and praise for our days
'Neath the sun, 'neath the stars, 'neath the sky
As we go, this we know
God is nigh.

A half-hour later, we companions returned to where Ken had been left. He was no longer napping or alone. He was engulfed by a large group of people with radiant smiles who were listening with rapt attention to Ken's tales. Visitors from around the world asked questions using the little English they knew. Surprisingly, Ken was usually able to comprehend at least some of their inquiries. The one question nearly everyone asked was whether he had served in General George S. Patton's Army. Patton was, and is, highly revered in France. He had helped liberate the country not once, but twice. In World War I, he proved to be a brilliant commander for the newly commissioned U.S. Tank Corps. During World War II, he is credited with liberating more French territory than any other Allied general. His Third Army killed, wounded, or captured more enemy soldiers than any army in recorded history during their relentless march across France and into Germany.

Patton had an affinity for France as well. He was fluent in its language and understood the culture, after having spent many years there. He had a voracious appetite for war history, particularly that of France. Due to fervent study, he possessed great knowledge of military history and doctrine. That knowledge paid off. Patton famously said, "It takes brains and guts to win wars. A man with guts but no brains is only half a soldier." He, and the men who had served with him, most certainly evidenced both.

Numerous monuments and statues across France express the enduring affection and gratitude the people hold for the general. Our team saw such a tribute in the town of Avranches, where Patton broke through the German Panzer counter-offensive on July 31, 1944, and headed west toward liberation of the Brittany Peninsula. Then, with lightning speed, he began to push the enemy east toward Paris. He eventually forced a retreat to the French/German border, where the war stalled for several months due to lack of supplies. (This was when Ken met Marguerite.) Patton Square in Avranches contains a towering memorial to this stalwart leader, a bronze bust of the general, and an American Sherman tank such as those used in the breakthrough. The square officially sits on our territory. American soil and trees were actually transported across the Atlantic to serve as a backdrop.

By their approving nods, the crowd seemed pleased to hear that Ken had indeed been under Patton's command, that he had delivered orders from him, and had even seen and heard the general on a couple of occasions (although you will recall Ken's displeasure at Patton's language—a rather "colorful" reflection of this audacious, complex man).

Individuals in turn shared their stories, embraced Ken, and posed for photographs with him. One Frenchman told how an American soldier had hidden in his grandmother's house while Nazis searched the area. He was later able to steal away into the night. Another said it was a pleasure to shake Ken's hand. His parents had been saved by American soldiers when Sainte-Mère-Église was liberated and, subsequently, he was born. A Belgian soldier explained how he had been a POW in Germany until he was saved by the Americans. He simply said, "Thank you that I am free." Schoolgirls from Holland were excited to have their picture taken with Ken, and another group from Italy clamored for his autograph.

Ken enjoyed meeting a fellow soldier, Arnold Whittaker, from Patton's 3rd Army, 5th Infantry Division, who also had a memoir published about his life entitled, *Foxhole Promises*. They greeted each other with hearty handshakes and proceeded to swap war stories. Mr. Whittaker, too, was honored yet humbled by the attention paid to him by the French and others at the cemetery. He had simply done what his country asked of him and was happy to have played a role. (We were sad to learn he passed away less than a year after their meeting at the age of 86.)

One especially touching moment came when a young French boy of five or six years, with chocolate brown eyes and hair, emerged from the crowd and quietly approached Ken. The child's mother sweetly asked whether her son could give him a hug. Ken, of course, obliged. The boy reached up and placed a tiny hand on one cheek, then gave him a gentle kiss on the other. The entire crowd was moved by this loving gesture: Ken simply melted.

In the distance, the mournful wail of bagpipes could be heard. The audience began to say its goodbyes to Ken, and to move away in the direction of the music. Desiring to see the gravesites up close and to have a moment of quiet reflection, Ken started to wheel himself down the sidewalk leading to the burial grounds. He stopped on a concrete square where the American flag was positioned.

Grateful to be alone, he looked out across the lawn. He took note of the striking geometric pattern of the crosses, and the vivid contrast of white against green against blue—a combination that elicited a surprising sense of serenity and order in a place that had known unspeakable terror and chaos. A handful of visitors ambled slowly among the crosses, pausing here and there to read the names of the fallen, or to place a flower or flag near a marker. There were few sounds other than the flapping of the flag, the distinctive melody of a song thrush, and the swish of the surf in the distance. Ken bowed his head, prayed, and wept in remembrance of those who lie in silence.

The clear, triumphant notes of *"La Marseillaise"* interrupted his thoughts. He looked across the landscape and saw that a huge throng had gathered around a flagpole square. Once the bugler, a member of the Royal Artillery, had finished the French march on his cornet, the doleful sound of the bagpipes, played by a member of the Highland regiment, started up again. Then the group began moving in unison along the sidewalk of the mall, following the bagpiper. Ken looked up to see an empty pole and realized they must have been participating in the lowering of the French flag. Now the huge entourage was descending upon the American flag—right near where he was sitting! Greg, Troy, and I, who were spread out around the grounds, realized it as well simultaneously. We all sprinted toward Ken, with cameras ready, and quickly wheeled him closer to the square.

The bagpiper strode across the mall and stopped not far from Ken. Several dignitaries and hundreds of spectators formed a semi-circle around the flag. The team was thankful to be able to witness the honoring of our flag and the principles for which it stands during the commemoration of D-Day. The moment was made even more special knowing that they were right at Omaha Beach where those principles had been "tried with fire." Then, out of the blue, quite literally, a USAF C-130 aircraft roared overhead during a flyover, briefly stealing the crowd's attention.

Next, four fit young men who were wearing colorful jerseys with the words "Big Battlefield Bike Ride" displayed across the front walked up to Ken single file. They smiled warmly and shook his hand before joining officials from the United States Air Force Academy, who were lined up to conduct the flag ceremony. A second plane soared overhead, thrilling the crowd once again. Then the master of ceremonies explained how it was customary for any military personnel to offer a salute while the flag was being lowered, and that any citizen of the United States in attendance should place their right hand over their heart. Everyone complied and stood quietly at attention. Just as the bugler was about to begin playing "Taps," the MC stopped the ceremony cold.

He paused a minute, then made an announcement that stunned our team and delighted the crowd. "Ladies and gentlemen, I must apologize for not recognizing this earlier. I have just learned that we have an American WWII veteran who served in Normandy with us this evening." All of a sudden, Ken felt himself being pushed up closer to the proceedings. The MC walked over to him, placed a hand on Ken's shoulder, and shook his hand vigorously while thanking him for his service to both nations. Ken could hardly believe his ears! How in the world had he heard of this old soldier? Ken looked up and was so surprised that he could do nothing but nod and shake the official's hand in return.

The MC resumed his position and the ceremony. Our flag, billowing gently in the salty breeze, was slowly lowered and gathered together. The bagpipes started up again, as soon as "Old Glory" was down, but its strains quickly faded as the piper left the square and slowly made his way toward the sea. The group began to carefully fold the flag lengthwise three times directly in front of Ken. Then one of the four young men who had greeted Ken stepped forward and solemnly began to create a neat triangle, folding the cloth hand over hand. As Ken was watching him work, he noticed that there was something different about all four of the men—each of them was missing one or both legs.

The young man firmly tucked in the final corner of the flag and handed it to the master of ceremonies. He clutched it to his chest, and then was expected to hand it back to the four men who had been designated as the honored recipients. Instead, as God's final gift to Ken on this trip, the MC spun around, marched forward, and extending his arms, offered it to the astounded Minnesota veteran. Ken's heart began to throb and he sensed an enormous, proverbial lump rising in his throat. With trembling hands, he reached up to receive it—the precious symbol of his nation for which untold millions had given their lives. The sheer heft of the flag was felt in his arms. The sheer weight of this moment was felt in his heart.

Ken gave a salute with tears slipping down his cheeks. The crowd erupted with applause as the ceremony concluded, with many in attendance wiping away tears of their own. The four men approached Ken again and shook his hand, profusely thanking him for serving during World War II. Realizing they were most likely veterans from the wars in Iraq and Afghanistan, Ken protested, "No, no, thank *you*! You really paid a price. I'm so proud of you guys." The young veterans gathered around Ken, each holding onto a corner of the flag, while dozens of people snapped pictures. The visitors then waited in line once again to express their appreciation for all the American heroes.

Ken deemed himself undeserving of such attention. These soldiers had been through unimaginable agony in losing limbs, yet they were intent on thanking Ken. He and our team were moved to tears by their humility, kindness, display of respect, and selflessness—even more so when we later learned that the handsome young men with prosthetic legs had noticed Ken mere minutes before the ceremony, and immediately requested that the flag be presented to him, rather than to them as planned.

The Iraq and Afghanistan vets were in France raising money for Help for Heroes, an independent British charity, which supports rehabilitative and therapeutic programs for wounded veterans. The organization, along with its U.S. counterpart, Operation Comfort, sponsors a 5-day, 320-mile bike tour called The Big Battlefield Bike Ride. Riders from around the world, plus teams of disabled veterans often using hand-pedaled bicycles, re-trace the route Allied forces took from the Normandy beaches to Paris, ending at the Eiffel Tower. In addition to fundraising, the veterans participate in wreath-laying ceremonies along the bike route at various military cemeteries in honor of the missing and the fallen.

Ken and the vets were swarmed again by well-wishers, while a final fly-over by the two C-130s signaled an end to the commemoration time and the closing of the cemetery. Visitors slowly began to make their way to the exit, some giving a final smile and wave to Ken. Several people lingered, perhaps seeking one last moment to pray, to remember, to express gratitude for the soldiers who had given their all. "Let me not mourn for the men who have died, but rather let me be glad that such heroes lived"—George S. Patton.

After the crowds had left, Ken sat for quite some time gazing at the markers. Several now had small bouquets of flowers or American flags at their bases as loving tributes. He began to ask himself impossible questions. How many men lying beneath the crosses were ones he had met, trained alongside, traveled with, ate with, laughed with, or prayed with? Why was he not among them? Why had he been blessed with a long life, a loving spouse, and children, grandchildren and great-grandchildren, while many of his compatriots had drawn their last breath at Normandy at an average age of just twenty-two years?

Such questions are hard to ask and even harder to answer. Yet Ken knew deep in his heart that the answers to all of life's most vexing questions are found in the Bible. He recalled what the psalmist says: "All the days ordained for me were written in your book before one of them came to be" (Psalm 139:16). God, who is infinitely good, wise, and loving, records our existence. He has predestined the day of our birth, the day of our death, and everything in-between. At birth, God knew us before He even formed us in the womb. In death, we who have been redeemed will be at home with Him forever. In all the "in-between," God works out His perfect plan for us, for our joy and His glory. In believing this, Ken could accept, embrace, and be thankful for the paths that God had determined for him—even the one that had led him so very far away from his beloved Marguerite.

Chapter Ten

Plein de Tristesse, mais Toujours Joyeux

Three years after having returned from France, Ken sits in his worn, comfortable chair in the living room of his 1970s rambler. Books, videos, model cars, and mementos are piled up on every available surface and sprinkled with more than one layer of dust. Family photos, greeting cards from Christmases long ago, pictures from old calendars, and yellowed pages torn from coloring books with "I love you Grandpa" scrawled along the bottom are tacked to the walls. From the perspective of the casual visitor, the room appears to be filled with clutter. From Ken's, it is filled with priceless treasures.

Among the wall decorations are two newer treasures—one is a framed letter congratulating Ken on his new title as a *Chevalier de la Légion d'Honneur,* or Knight of the French Legion of Honor. This is France's highest military distinction. It was created by Napoléon Bonaparte in 1802, and is usually reserved for French nationals who have made outstanding contributions to their country. The French government has begun bestowing this honor on select American soldiers, as well, in recognition of their heroic efforts in liberating France during World War II.

In February of 2012, a decoration ceremony was held at the Minnesota State Capitol building in St. Paul for Ken and another Minnesota veteran, John Teman, who has since passed away. John was a highly decorated 2nd Lieutenant and C-47 pilot in the 439th Transport Carrier Group. With their families and friends, the media, and hundreds of Minnesotans looking on, Ken and John were presented with the prestigious medals. They also received certificates signed by then President Nicolas Sarkosy on behalf of the French people.

The second frame holds a newspaper article and photograph highlighting another special event. Several weeks after having received the French medal, Ken was asked to appear before the Minnesota House of Representatives. Each year, members of the House are given the opportunity to choose a local citizen to be recognized in the House chamber. Ken's state representative, Tim Sanders, had heard of his constituent's military service and invited him to be the designee. Ken was flabbergasted. He had not been down to the State Capitol since he was a school child, and here he was being honored there twice in one year. Following a brief ceremony, the legislators rose and then approached Ken to greet him personally. The Minnesota veteran proved to be a charmer, as usual, with his twinkling blue eyes, warm smile, and good sense of humor. Representative Sanders exclaimed that he had never witnessed so many House members lined up to shake an honoree's hand.

The awards he had received were priceless to Ken, but

he was well aware that one day they would all fade away. Ken's jaw dropped when he learned that he may possess a more *permanent* souvenir from the war, however. After having had three MRIs performed to diagnose an eye problem, Ken's ophthalmologist asked him repeatedly whether he had any metal in his head. Ken was adamant that he had none to his knowledge, yet the tests clearly showed the presence of metal, other than that of the silver and gold in his teeth.

Ken had been wracking his brain trying to guess where he may have acquired it, when it dawned on him: one day while in France, Ken had been riding in a jeep with three buddies. They came upon another vehicle overflowing with confiscated German weapons, which were free for the taking. One soldier grabbed a luger, examined it, and passed it to the GI sitting behind Ken. German lugers, 9mm semi-automatic pistols, were highly prized by Allied soldiers as war trophies. Ken nearly jumped out of his skin when he heard an ear-piercing pop right next to him. Feeling a hit just under his helmet, he thought he had been shot. He instinctively slapped his hand to his neck, but surprisingly, there was neither pain nor blood. Relieved, Ken figured he had been merely grazed by the shell casing.

Ken turned around to where his buddy was sitting. He was shocked to see blood spurting from the stunned soldier's leg—he had accidentally shot himself. The bullet had gone clean through his calf and into the floorboards of the jeep. The driver took one look at his buddy's soggy, scarlet pant leg and ashen face, and then sped to an aid station run by the Second French Armored Division. The staff quickly assessed the injury and began treating it. No anesthetic was available as the medics dug out bits of mangled flesh.

The soldier groaned not only at the excruciating pain, but also at his utter stupidity. After being stabilized, he was sent away for additional treatment. Ken never saw him again. He wondered if the irony of having shot himself with an enemy weapon—the same sort he had been diligently dodging these many months— had ever struck the sorry soldier. Ken was curious now as to whether a sliver of shrapnel had penetrated his skin. Had a souvenir of the war been lodged in his head all these years, accounting for the MRI results?

In Ken's lap sits his mail—the usual assortment of bills and ads—but one white envelope snatches his attention as he riffles through the pile. The letter has a foreign postmark. At long last, it is a letter from Lisa. She and her family had moved west to Paris many months ago, and Ken had been curious about their adjustment to the new home. He slices open the top of the letter with a sharp knife and a shaky hand and begins to read.

Aside from the usual pleasantries, there is amazing news—Tim, Lisa, and the children who are now eight and ten years old are planning to spend a month in the United States. Their first stop is Minnesota! Lisa explains that she has imagined Ken's homeland since she was a dreamy teenager, mooning over her great-aunt's heart-rending love story. Having been intent on seeing it, she and Tim have placed Minnesota as a priority on their itinerary. It would be the first trip to America for their children and a fantasy fulfilled for Lisa. They would finally visit Ken in his home and meet the family known only through words and photographs.

Ken is dizzy with happiness: he had been dreaming for years that Lisa would come to see him. His mind begins to race. Ken immediately contemplates what he will need to do to prepare for his guests, despite the fact that they will not arrive for months. His "bachelor pad" will require a good purging and scrubbing, the threadbare sheets in the spare bedroom will need replacing, and what about the meals? It will be a challenge to compete with the likes of authentic Quiche Lorraine and Crème Brulée. Undaunted, Ken ponders his own special recipes for creamy potato salad and blueberry pie, and begins to make a mental grocery list. He was treated like a king in France, and is determined to give his guests the royal treatment—Minnesota style—as well.

At the same time he is gleefully making plans, Ken senses a vague heaviness in his heart. He tries to ignore it, but it grows steadily and threatens to crush the peace he had received at the foot of Margie's grave. Its source is well-known—the still-painful reality that Margie is gone. Refusing to let grief overwhelm him again, Ken clings to the fact that God knows our sorrows. The Bible says He keeps track of them and even collects all our tears in His bottle. Ken had certainly contributed his share.

God does not simply amass the bitter tears of our lives, however. He promises to heal the broken-hearted and assures us that although weeping endures for the night, joy comes in the morning. For Ken, returning to Fénétrange had finally brought the morning. Simply standing before Marguerite's grave and saying he was sorry allowed Ken to forgive himself.

Now it was time for joy—joy in having experienced Margie's love and comfort during a pivotal time in his life. Joy in believing that he would see her once again in Heaven. Joy in knowing that he had kept his word—he had gone back. Sitting in his chair he smiles, forever thankful that it had *not* been too late to fulfill his promise and to whisper his very last words to her—"I never stopped loving you."

Ken leaves for France—May 2011

Eiffel Tower

Ken's view from the Tower

Seine River

Père Lachaise Cemetery

Ken and the French General

Tomb of the Unknown—Paris

Ken under the Arch of Triumph

Friendly French cows

Sunset in the country

Château d'Alteville—Tarquimpol

Lunéville Bridge

Jean, Vianne, Ken

Marthe's g

Charles' painting

Charles, Ken, Marth

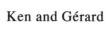
Ken and Gérard

Gérard

Charles, Lili, Jean-Pierre

Ken and Lili

Ken at the Molsheim Cemetery

Lee, Ken at the archway
to the Castle

étrange Castle in 1944

The Castle in 2011

The Klein Home

Ken and Charles

Ken and the "smooching bench"

Ken's bedroom window

U.S. Army Headquarters
—Fénétrange

Fénétrange Castle
on the Saar River

Frédéric's tools, wheel

"Ken and Margie's" meadow

Original railroad tracks
to Fénétrange

Lee, Troy at the
Fénétrange station

Fénétrange train station

Fénétrange Town Hall

nd the Mayor of Fénétrange

Ken and his honorary hat and pin

eople of Fénétrange

Ken visits Margie's Church

House in Alsace

Ken's adventure with Greg and Troy

me

Sherman tank near Strasbourg

Ill River—Strasbourg

Mont St. Michel

Strasbourg Cathedral

"Iron Mike" statue—
La Fière Memorial Park

Ken's jeep ride

Ken and the "Tommy gun"

...nd the French reenactors

Mulberry Harbor off "Gold Beach" — Arromanches

D-Day Museum—Arromanches

German Bunker—Omaha B

Ken prays on Omaha Bea

Tribute at American
Cemetery—Colleville-sur-Me

Patton Square — Avranches

A sweet kiss

Ken meets American veterans
of Iraq War

Flag Ceremony—
American Cemetery
Colleville-sur-Mer*

Ken receives the
American flag*

American Cemetery—Colleville-sur-Mer

French Legion
Of Honor Medal

Ken in the Minnesota House Chamber

Ken greets the
Minnesota House
of Representatives

Jean, Lisa,
Vianne, Tim,
Ken